Aldous Huxley

Titles in the series Critical Lives present the work of leading cultural figures of the modern period. Each book explores the life of the artist, writer, philosopher or architect in question and relates it to their major works.

Aldous Huxley

Jake Poller

REAKTION BOOKS

For Ayako

Published by
REAKTION BOOKS LTD
Unit 32, Waterside
44–48 Wharf Road
London N1 7UX, UK

www.reaktionbooks.co.uk

First published 2021
Copyright © Jake Poller 2021

Printed and bound in Great Britain by TJ Books Ltd, Padstow, Cornwall

A catalogue record for this book is available from the British Library

ISBN 978 1 78914 427 7

Contents

Abbreviations

Publicity photograph of Aldous Huxley, 1934.

Introduction: Island Universes

The work of Aldous Huxley is haunted by the notion of 'island universes'. In *The Devils of Loudun* (1952), he asserts that humans 'long to get out of themselves, to pass beyond the limits of that tiny island universe, within which every individual finds himself confined' (*DL*, 78). On one level, Huxley's longing for transcendence can be traced to his body. At the age of sixteen, an inflammation of the cornea permanently impaired his eyesight. As an adult, he was plagued by respiratory complaints and chose to live abroad as soon as he was able in order to avoid the brumous British winter, but even in the temperate climates of Italy, the south of France and California he was beset by influenza, bronchitis and pneumonia. His friend Gerald Heard wrote that 'Huxley's body hurt quite a lot most of the time; a little nearly all of the time; intensely, far too often.'[1] He was also dogged by eczema, hives and oedema and suffered from piles in his twenties. It was because of his beleaguered body that he pursued such (at the time) unconventional treatments as the Alexander technique, the Bates method and colonic irrigation and submitted to faddish diets.

Huxley put great stock in the American psychologist William Sheldon's psycho-physical classification, and believed it explained many things about his personality. Sheldon identified three body types: the soft fat endomorph, the large-boned muscular mesomorph, and the small-boned lanky ectomorph. These body types were correlated with three temperaments: viscerotonia is characterized by love of food, company and ceremony; somatotonia is associated with 'love of muscular activity, aggressiveness and lust for power'; while cerebrotonia is marked by nervousness, shyness and introversion. Huxley classified himself as a 'cerebrotonic ectomorph', a type he described in passing as 'almost insanely sexual' as a result of their 'over-sensitiveness' (*PP*, 149–50). Given his Sheldonian classification, it is perhaps no surprise that Huxley attempted to transcend the island universe of himself through sex, but libidinousness, as can be seen from his satirical early fiction, only led to loneliness and jealousy. Indeed, part of Huxley's early reputation derived from his frank treatment of sexuality and his depiction of hedonistic flappers whose restless promiscuity was an index of their anomie.

The second sense of the 'island universe' is one of social isolation. In *The Doors of Perception* (1954), he writes:

> We live together, we act on, and react to, one another; but always and in all circumstances we are by ourselves. The martyrs go hand in hand into the arena; they are crucified alone. Embraced, the lovers desperately try to fuse their insulated ecstasies into a single self-transcendence; in vain . . . From family to nation, every human group is a society of island universes. (*DP*, 11–12)

Throughout his work, Huxley acutely chronicled the frustration, confusion and humour that arise from social interactions. After a comic misunderstanding with the hearing-impaired Jenny Mullion in *Crome Yellow* (1921), the young poet Denis Stone reflects: 'Did one ever establish contact with anyone? We are all parallel straight lines' (*CY*, 15). Another significant feature of cerebrotonia that chimed with Huxley was a distaste for displays of emotion and an almost total inability to communicate one's feelings. This made him a terrible father and, at least with his first wife Maria, a fairly indifferent husband. In his diary Christopher Isherwood recorded

Gerald Heard as confiding 'that Maria, just before she died, told him that she had no idea if Aldous really loved her or not'.[2] It is worth noting, though, that Heard had a highly competitive friendship with Huxley, and consequently he – and the bitchy Isherwood for that matter – cannot be completely trusted.

The third sense of the 'island universe' relates to the phenomenal world, to 'one damned thing after the other', as Huxley sometimes put it. In the poetry anthology *Texts and Pretexts* (1932), he writes: 'Our experience is divided up into island universes. We jump from one to the other – there are no bridges.'[3] Huxley is contrasting this sense of everything being isolated and unconnected to the 'all feeling' of mysticism, in which the multiplicity of the world is revealed as the surface illusion of a much greater, deeper unity. The phrase 'island universe' originated with Immanuel Kant, who back in the eighteenth century speculated that the cloudy objects (spiral nebulae or 'island universes', as Kant dubbed them) observed by astronomers could be other galaxies. At the time the Milky Way was considered to be the *only* galaxy, and it was not until 1923 that Edwin Hubble was able to confirm that these island universes did indeed lie outside the Milky Way.[4] Never had the universe, which had just increased in size exponentially, seemed more awesome. Huxley would come to conceive of the cosmos, and everything in the cosmos, from atoms to ants to human beings and stars, as an emanation from the divine Ground of Being. He believed that mystics made contact with this godhead, the divine Ground, and from this ineffable experience they derived teachings that bore a genealogical resemblance to the teaching of mystics from different eras and religious traditions. The implication being that these otherwise disparate mystics had an experience of the same godhead, rather than an exclusively Christian, Jewish or Muslim God.

During the Second World War Huxley compiled an anthology of these mystical teachings that he titled *The Perennial Philosophy* (1945). From 1935 onwards, he hoped that mysticism would furnish him with a bridge between his island self and the rest of the world. But while he attempted to lead a more ascetic lifestyle and practised meditation, he had to wait another two decades until, under the influence of mescaline, he was able to experience this cosmic unity for himself. Mescaline afforded him the perfect means of self-transcendence. There was a collapse of conventional subject–object dualism. In the mystical phase of the psychedelic experience, Huxley writes, 'the world is now seen as an infinite diversity that is yet a unity, and the beholder experiences himself as being one with the infinite Oneness that manifests itself, totally present, at every point of space, at every instant in the flux of perpetual perishing and perpetual renewal.'[5] Psychedelic drugs also helped Huxley to overcome his emotional allergy. In a mescaline experiment from 1955, not long after Maria's death, he handed his guide Laura Archera (who would become his second wife) a piece of paper on which he had written: 'I want to know, and constantly be in, the state of love.'[6] In a letter to the psychiatrist Humphry Osmond, he writes that during this trip he was able to experience 'love as the primary and fundamental cosmic fact' (*LAH*, 769). In a subsequent session the following year, he was finally able to weep over Maria's death and that of his mother, who had died of cancer when he was fourteen.

Huxley also used the term 'island universes' as a metaphor for different and often incommensurable varieties of knowledge. In the novel *Time Must Have a Stop* (1944), the narrator refers to the 'island universes of discourse' (*TMHS*, 270). Huxley often complained that academics knew a great deal about their own specialisms, but almost nothing about the other island universes outside their field. As an author and essayist, Huxley saw his role as a bridge-builder between these different island universes, and made a conscientious effort to stay abreast of scientific developments as well as literature and the arts, parapsychology as well as psychiatry, the new physics and metaphysics. Huxley came from a formidable line of educators. His father Leonard Huxley had been an assistant master at Charterhouse School. His mother Julia Arnold had single-handedly established the Prior's Field School in Godalming, Surrey, and served as its headmistress. Julia was the niece of the poet and essayist Matthew Arnold and the granddaughter of Thomas Arnold, the headmaster of Rugby School and one of Lytton Strachey's eminent Victorians. Huxley's grandfather, the renowned scientist T. H. Huxley, held a number of different teaching posts, including professor of biology at the Normal School of Science, where he exerted a great influence on H. G. Wells. Huxley's sister Margaret would also found her own school in Bexhill, Sussex, with her partner Christabel Mumford.

This is a comparatively brief 'Critical Life' of Huxley, and I've had to leave out quite a bit of his extensive oeuvre. Huxley published six volumes of poetry, but I only analyse a small selection. However, I believe that his poetry has not been unjustly neglected; it lacks the affecting simplicity of D. H. Lawrence at his best (I'm thinking here of 'The Ship of Death'), or the astounding, wrong-footing originality of W. B. Yeats ('That dolphin-torn, that gong-tormented sea'). Huxley's essays, on the other hand, deserve a much wider readership. He published eight essay collections in his lifetime but composed countless others for a wide array of magazines, newspapers and journals, and his *Complete Essays* run to six unwieldy volumes. Consequently, I have only been able to touch on a handful of his essays. This is a pity as Huxley's great gift as a writer was not for storytelling or characterization but for the lucid exposition of ideas, and as such the essay was the perfect vehicle for his talent. He often lamented that he was not a 'born novelist' but was able 'to simulate a novelist's behaviour not too unconvincingly'. This failing was due, he believed, to his ectomorphic body, for he notes that the most fertile novelists who painted on a broad social canvas were all 'burly genial fellows', in other words viscerotonic endomorphs, such as Tolstoy, Balzac and Dickens (*LAH*, 516). Huxley also wrote plays and published five volumes of short stories and three books of travel writing, but space does not permit more than a glancing examination of them.

The present book is not the only biography of Huxley. Inevitably, each biographer offers a variegated portrait of Huxley that is inflected by her own interests and idiosyncrasies. I am indebted to Sybille Bedford's two-volume life of Huxley, but Bedford would never have revealed that she was Maria's lover while they both lived in Sanary-sur-Mer in the south of France; nor that Bedford's friend and former lover, the artist Eva Herrmann, slept with Huxley. Bedford also chose to omit Huxley's affair with the socialite Mary Hutchinson. Fortunately, I do not share Bedford's aristocratic German politesse. David King Dunaway's biography, *Huxley in Hollywood* (1989), is very good on the America years (1937–63). Nicholas Murray did some magnificent archival work in his 2002 biography, for instance fishing up the affair with Hutchinson. But I think it is fair to say that neither Bedford, Dunaway nor Murray possessed a scholarly understanding of the subjects of mysticism and alternative spirituality – without which, I believe, a nuanced understanding of Huxley's work is impossible. The professor of religion Dana Sawyer wrote with authority and sympathy about Huxley's vacillating spiritual interests in his 2002 biography, but did not examine his fiction in any depth. The distinguishing feature of this biography is that I have devoted an equal amount of space to the life and the work. Given the perennial pertinence and profundity of Huxley's thinking, I very much doubt my biography will be the last.

1

Bildung and *Roman*, 1894–1921

Aldous Leonard Huxley was born on 26 July 1894 in Godalming, Surrey, in the twilight of the Victorian era. His father, Leonard Huxley, was an old-fashioned man of letters. In 1901 he joined the publishing firm of Smith, Elder & Co., where he helped to edit the *Cornhill Magazine*, which was named after the publisher's address at 65 Cornhill, London. Leonard wrote biographies of his father, T. H. Huxley, and the botanist and explorer Joseph Dalton Hooker; edited editions of the letters of Jane Welsh Carlyle and Elizabeth Barrett Browning; and became editor of the *Cornhill* in 1916. In 1885 he married Julia Frances Arnold, the sister of the novelist Mrs Humphry Ward. Julia had obtained a first in English Literature from Somerville College, Oxford, and went on to found Prior's Field School. By the time of Aldous's birth she already had two sons, Julian and Trevenen, while her youngest child was a daughter, Margaret.

Huxley attended Prior's Field and was deeply devoted to his mother. At his prep school, Hillside, he was a popular pupil and forged lasting friendships with his cousin Gervas Huxley and Lewis Gielgud (whose brother John would become a famous actor). At the end of November 1908, while Huxley was in his first term at Eton, his mother died of cancer. Julia was just 46 and had only been seriously ill for a couple of months.[1] This was the first of three tragedies that blighted Huxley's childhood and youth. At Eton, Huxley had begun to demonstrate his intellectual aptitude: he

Thomas Henry and Julian Huxley (Aldous's grandfather and brother, respectively),
c. 1895.

excelled at English and science, and by the age of sixteen he had decided to become a doctor, honouring the scientific legacy of his grandfather T. H. Huxley and his brother Julian, who was studying Natural Science at the University of Oxford.

In the winter of 1910–11, Huxley contracted keratitis punctata, an inflammation of the cornea, which left him almost totally blind for a period of about eighteen months. This had the effect, Huxley would later write, of greatly reinforcing his 'natural tendency towards solitude and away from practical matters' (*LAH*, 473). It is no coincidence that it was during this period that he wrote his first novel, now lost, about 'a young man and his relationship to two different kind[s] of women', which Huxley recalled in 1961 as being 'bitter' in tone.[2] He may have turned to fiction through boredom (he had to use a guide to walk and was largely confined to his room), or from a desire to escape the harrowing prospect of never regaining his sight, but he may also have recognized that his permanently impaired vision meant his proposed career in medicine was untenable. Unable to return to Eton, he was cared for by various relatives: his father in London (Leonard had moved to a house in Westbourne Square in 1909); his aunt, Mary Ward, at her home in Hertfordshire; and Ethel Collier in Swiss Cottage, the daughter of T. H. Huxley and wife of the portrait painter John Collier. Huxley stoically taught himself to read Braille and, with the help of private tutors, he was able to resume his education.

By March 1912 he could walk unaided and even contrived to ride a bike, despite the fact that, according to Gervas, 'he really couldn't see.'[3] With one eye, he was now able to read with the help of a magnifying glass, while the other was only capable of light perception. Somewhat surprisingly, for such an autobiographical writer, Huxley never fictionalized the experience and only briefly broached the subject in his book about the Bates method, *The Art of Seeing* (1942): 'My inability to see was mainly due to the presence of opacities in the cornea; but this condition was complicated by hyperopia and astigmatism.' After a couple of years, he was able to read with glasses, but was frequently 'overcome by that sense of complete physical and mental exhaustion which only eye-strain can produce'.[4] Around this time, Leonard (then 52) married Rosalind Bruce, who was thirty years his junior and even younger than Julian and Trevenen. It seems that Leonard was tactless in breaking the news and his comparatively hasty remarriage (three years after Julia's death) was greeted with consternation by his children.

Huxley travelled by himself to Marburg, Germany, in May 1912. Here he was the guest of Emanuel Kayser, a professor of geology. From his letters, it seems he spent much of his time taking German and piano lessons (he had taught himself to play by touch during the months of his blindness). His eyesight had recovered sufficiently for him to make several lively sketches of the local landscape and various German types, such as beer-drinking porters, students, marching musicians and policemen in Prussian uniforms. He also composed and illustrated several exuberant limericks, such as this:

The notorious Vasco da Gama
Possessed a one-legged pyjama,
Which was recently found
In a hole in the ground,
In the centre of North Alabama.[5]

The following year, Huxley spent some time in Oxford with his brother Trevenen. He was very attached to Trevenen, who was studying hard for his finals in Greats (that is, Classics) and held himself to a very high standard, both ethically and intellectually. Trevenen helped his brother prepare for the formidable Oxford entrance exam. In spite of his poor eyesight, Huxley had been reading widely and had developed an interest in the French symbolist poets. In order to work on his French, he spent July and August of 1913 in La Tronche, next to Grenoble.

Huxley's aunt, the novelist Mrs Humphry Ward.

Huxley went up to Oxford in October, having been offered a place at Balliol College, the alma mater of his brothers, his father and Matthew Arnold. He was studying for the newfangled degree in English Language and Literature, which, at the time, was regarded by the university as a rather frivolous subject, thus they felt it necessary to include a lot of Anglo-Saxon philology to lend the course academic heft. Huxley's letters from Balliol are punctuated with imprecations about having to read tedious Anglo-Saxon epics and sermons. At 6 feet 4½ inches, Huxley cut an impressive figure at Oxford. He had a thick brown mane of hair like his grandfather. He wore a homburg hat and dressed in three-piece suits. His right eye appeared cloudy and asquint, and was routinely concealed or touched up in his publicity photos. He was incredibly thin and, in combination with his height, this gave him a slightly gangling appearance – in subsequent caricatures, he would be depicted as a stick insect. By all accounts, Huxley had a wonderful first year at Oxford. Gervas Huxley and Lewis Gielgud went up at the same time, and he was friends with the biologist J.B.S. Haldane and his younger sister Naomi, who lived with her parents in Oxford.[6] He was also popular with the Balliol freshmen: he had a piano in his room on which he played ragtime and impressed his friends with erudite quotations – one of the benefits of his temporary blindness and reading with Braille was that it made him remember what he read.

But all was not well with his brother Trevenen, who had only achieved a second in Greats. Up until then, Trevenen had had much more academic success than Aldous. He had won prizes at Eton for Latin and mathematics as well as the Bryant Scholarship, and at Oxford had received a first for his Maths Mods (gruelling exams at the end of the first year).[7] In the wake of his second-class degree, Trevenen had failed the civil service examination. According to Francis Huxley (Julian's son), Leonard and Julia had instilled in their children the 'necessity of being large brains' after the fashion of their grandfather,[8] and Julian's stellar career at Oxford had only

Huxley in the Garden Quad, Balliol College, Oxford, *c.* 1915.

raised the bar. At a low ebb, with no job and feeling like a failure, Trevenen had begun an affair with one of the family's servants. According to Julian, Trevenen had attempted to educate the girl by taking her to the theatre, concerts and public lectures.[9] Huxley's first biographer, Sybille Bedford, notes that Trevenen 'had an ascetic streak, detesting jokes and boys' talk about sex, and [had] an inclination to subdue his instincts by his principles'.[10] He was therefore distressed that his love for the housemaid had a sexual component that he was not strong enough to resist. One of the family's faithful retainers knew about the affair and forced them to part, foreseeing that the girl would never be accepted in the Huxleys' social milieu. For Trevenen, the conflict engendered by this relationship and its painful break-up, added to the ignominy of his academic failure, culminated in a clinical depression and he was sent to a nursing home in Surrey to recuperate. While there, he received a letter from the girl informing him that she was pregnant.[11] This constituted the final blow for Trevenen, who hanged himself from a tree in the nearby woods.

Trevenen's suicide was the third tragedy of Huxley's formative years and the unforgiving satire and cynical assessments of human nature that mark his early work can be inferred as a response to these losses. Trevenen's puritanical attitude to sex was shared by his brother Julian, who had become engaged to a girl from Prior's Field, but his attraction to the girl was undermined by feelings of guilt and disgust, and he suffered a breakdown when she called it off. In retrospect, Julian blamed the sanctimonious morality of the Edwardian era, 'with its hypocritical suppression of everything "nasty"', for creating a conflict between the ego and the id, which had ruined his relationship.[12] Trevenen's predicament, being torn between a lofty spiritual love and the libidinal desires of the body, is treated in Huxley's sonnet sequence 'The Defeat of Youth' (1918) and would become a motif in his early work. The unnamed youth of the title cannot tolerate the coexistence of love and lust, and the poem's speaker describes the youth's sexual feelings as a 'hoofed obscenity' (*CP*, 47). His 'high love' for the girl is replaced by a 'dull rancorous fire' and he feels for her 'a fierce lust . . . more cruel than hate' (*CP*, 49). In the final sonnet of the sequence, the youth returns to the wood where he had fallen in love with the girl, in order to hang himself:

Tears of pain and shame,
And lips that once had laughed and sung and kissed
Trembling in the passion of his sobbing breath!
The world a candle shuddering to its death,
And life a darkness, blind and utterly void
Of any love or goodness: all deceit,
This friendship and this God: all shams destroyed,
And truth seen now.

Earth fails beneath his feet. (CP, 50)

In the same month as Trevenen's suicide, Britain entered the
First World War. By the time Huxley returned to Balliol in October,
most of his friends and fellow students had enlisted, leaving Oxford
deserted apart from international students such as T. S. Eliot and a
'crowd of painful young women' (*LAH*, 66). He was required to lodge
with the Haldane family (Huxley's friend John had enlisted) as there
were 250 soldiers billeted at Balliol. Huxley's early attitude to the war
was conventionally patriotic and he attempted to enlist three times
but was rejected due to his poor eyesight.[13] In his correspondence
from the period, there are jocular references to the 'Boches' and
'Boche-land', as well as belligerent comments about German culture.
But the mounting casualties of war and the influence of outspoken
pacifists such as Ottoline Morrell and Bertrand Russell led Huxley
to adopt a more sober, reflective stance.

Huxley first visited Garsington Manor, the Elizabethan home of
Lady Ottoline Morrell, on 28 November 1915. While Morrell initially
struck Huxley as absurdly affected, he soon became a regular
guest at Garsington, where he would meet many celebrated artists
and intellectuals, including Virginia Woolf, Katherine Mansfield,
Dorothy Brett, Dora Carrington, Clive Bell and Lytton Strachey, as
well as his future wife, the Belgian refugee Maria Nys. The following
year, he writes to Julian: 'The Morrell household is among the most
delightful I know: always interesting people there and v. good talk:

Huxley and Rupert Fellowes in the Fellows' Garden at Balliol College, Oxford, *c.* 1915.

I go over from Oxford often to see them.' The influence of Garsington and the pacifists can be glimpsed when Huxley writes, in the same letter: 'The longer this war goes on, the more one loathes and detests it. At the beginning I shd. have liked very much to fight: but now, if I could (having seen all the results), I think I'd be a conscientious objector, or nearly so' (*LAH*, 97).

It was at Morrell's urging that Huxley first made contact with D. H. Lawrence, who appears to have made a great impression on him, for he describes Lawrence to Julian as a 'novelist and poet and genius', whereas prior to their meeting in December 1915 Huxley had lampooned *The Rainbow*: 'the book is so dull that no one would under ordinary circumstances read it'; that is, if it hadn't been banned for obscenity (*LAH*, 85, 88). Lawrence was hoping to establish a utopian community in Florida and asked Huxley to join him. Huxley was planning a trip to Texas to visit Julian (who was teaching biology there at Rice University), so he promptly agreed, writing to Julian that a spell at Lawrence's community would be good for his soul.

It was around this time that Huxley developed an interest in mysticism. 'I have come to agree with Thomas Aquinas', he writes in December 1915, 'that individuality . . . is nothing more than a question of mere matter. We are potentially at least, though habit of matter has separated us, unanimous. One cannot escape mysticism; it positively thrusts itself, the only possibility, upon one' (*LAH*, 88). Mystics such as Aquinas were able to subsume their ego in, or unite it with, the godhead, a term which connotes an impersonal deity or universal mind (as opposed to an old man with a grey beard) that both transcends and is immanent in the cosmos.

Ottoline Morrell (standing) and guests at Garsington, including Lytton Strachey (seated with a beard and glasses), Mary Hutchinson to his left, Clive Bell to her left and Juliette Baillot seated on the ground with an alice band.

What Huxley is getting at in the quotation above is that while we appear to be individuals, due to our physically isolated selves, the mystic perceives that on a deeper level individuality and isolation are an illusion, since we (and everything else for that matter) are an emanation of the godhead. This mystical cosmology can be contrasted with Christianity, in which a personal God creates the world *ex nihilo*, rather than out of his divine being, and therefore the world is fallen. Broadly speaking, there are two types of mystical experience, which the philosopher W. T. Stace termed 'introvertive' and 'extrovertive'. In the former, the mystic turns away from the phenomenal world, usually in meditation, and experiences a state of 'undifferentiated unity' with the 'One' or godhead; in the latter (also known as 'nature mysticism' and 'cosmic consciousness'), the mystic turns her gaze outwards but apprehends that behind the ostensible multiplicity of the phenomenal world all things are One, and the mystic is included in this unifying vision.[14] While introvertive experience is most often reported by religious figures, such as Aquinas and St John of the Cross, laypeople are susceptible to extrovertive experience. In his letters, Huxley sometimes expresses a feeling of mystical oneness with nature – 'One does feel tremendously, when one is in this beautiful country [Scotland], that one is part of a larger soul, which embraces everything' (*LAH*, 73) – but these are intimations rather than episodes of extrovertive experience, and Huxley would have to wait until his first mescaline experiment in 1953 to enjoy the latter in its psychedelic fullness.

In his final year at Oxford, Huxley returned to a new room at Balliol. He and some friends launched a quarterly magazine called the *Palatine Review*, in which Huxley published poetry, short stories and reviews. On the strength of his poem 'Mole' in the first issue (February 1916), Huxley was invited by the editor of the *Nation* to submit some poems for publication, but these would bathetically appear under the name Leonard Huxley, with his father being praised by friends for his beautiful verse. Huxley left

Oxford in high spirits, having gained a first in his finals and won the Stanhope Prize for an essay on satire; he had also had a volume of poetry, *The Burning Wheel* (1916), accepted for publication. While other poets, such as Eliot and Ezra Pound, were at this time trying to 'make it new' by experimenting with form and free verse, Huxley's poetry was scrupulously traditional. The majority of the poems contained in *The Burning Wheel* are sonnets, and the rest of them use rhyme and a recognizable metre, with the exception of the title poem. Huxley had been reading a lot of mystical works, in particular William Blake and Jacob Boehme. The latter was a Lutheran shoemaker who in 1600 underwent a profound mystical experience that left him with the conviction that God, far from being sequestered in heaven, was in fact everywhere. Huxley later stated that the title poem 'The Burning Wheel' derived from Boehme,[15] whose complex and voluminous work defies easy summary, but suffice it to say that Boehme wrote about a 'wheel of nature' and a 'wheel of anguish' and these can be linked to the Buddhist *bhavachakra* (wheel of *samsara* or rebirth) and the 'wheel' or circle of the ouroboros (the serpent eating its own tail), all of which refer to time and eternity, death and rebirth, creation and destruction. 'Wearied of its own turning', the burning wheel 'must strain through agony / On agony' in order to return to its 'adamant core' (oneness, death). But the wheel never stops turning, with a new flame 'Billowing out' to the circumference (multiplicity, rebirth), only to retreat into the oneness of the centre (*cp*, 15–16).

In July 1916 Huxley picked up half a term's teaching at Repton School in Derby, but he felt lonely amid the complacent middle-aged masters and missed the badinage of his friends. In September, after desultorily searching for other teaching jobs, he elected to work on the farm at Garsington alongside conscientious objectors, such as the art critic Clive Bell and Bertrand Russell. Although conscription had been introduced at the start of the year, Huxley had been attested by the military as unfit so he never had to identify himself as a conscientious objector. At Garsington, he seems to have been chiefly employed in cutting down trees for firewood and found the work congenial. 'I find it a very pleasant process', he writes, 'quite annihilating the inconveniences of mental activity . . . *Non cogito, ergo sum felix*' (*SL*, 39).

Huxley's courtship and engagement to Maria are conspicuously absent from his letters. Maria was from an affluent Belgian family: her mother and three younger sisters had come to England at the outbreak of the First World War. Maria's uncle was the painter George Baltus,[16] who arranged for Maria to stay with Ottoline Morrell. In the autumn of 1915 Maria was sent to Newnham College, Cambridge, and she does not appear in Huxley's published letters until July 1916. In one of Huxley's few surviving diaries, Maria makes an appearance in April 1916: 'Maria and [Dora] Carrington bathed' in the ornamental pond at Garsington: 'a delightfully nymph-like scene'.[17] The following day, Huxley took a dip in the pond with Maria and afterwards they sunbathed on the roof. But at this time Maria was in love with Morrell. The previous year (April 1915), fearing that Morrell would send her away to study rather than letting her come to Garsington (Maria had been residing at Morrell's London home in Bedford Square), Maria attempted suicide.[18] She was just sixteen at the time, petite (five feet) and still shedding the puppy fat of her adolescence, whereas Morrell was married, 42 years old and emphasized her height (she was almost six feet tall) by wearing heels and elevators. After Morrell's death in 1938, Maria would describe her love for Morrell as the 'greatest' of her life.[19] Meanwhile, Maria was not the only girl at Garsington who appealed to Huxley. In her memoirs, Morrell writes that in the summer of 1916 Huxley 'seemed to be rather in love with Carrington'.[20]

While Huxley was chopping wood at Garsington, Maria was largely absent. She returned to Newnham in October for her second year, only to be sent down two weeks later as her academic work didn't pass muster. She then became a resident at 'the Ark' in

Gower Street, the house of the economist John Maynard Keynes, which was being rented by Dorothy Brett, Dora Carrington, Katherine Mansfield and John Middleton Murry.[21] Bedford asserts that Huxley proposed to Maria on the lawn of Garsington, but does not specify when, so presumably this must have occurred prior to Maria's departure in October.[22] Nicholas Murray opines that the proposal took place in the summer but was kept secret from family and friends, which is why it is absent from his correspondence.[23] Huxley writes to Morrell in October that he has a 'doggy devotion' to Maria (*sl*, 40), which is a pretty prosaic formula to use about one's fiancée. He went down to London frequently to see Maria, who was making ends meet by giving French lessons. They both spent Christmas at Garsington, but Philip Morrell objected to Maria living there;[24] Brett was tired of looking after her in the Ark; and with Huxley unable to support her, she was sent back to her mother, who was now living in Florence, in January 1917.

Morrell reports that after Maria's departure, Huxley was despondent and bombarded her with letters while Maria wrote to him infrequently and appeared to be fine without him. Moreover, Maria's love for Morrell still clearly eclipsed her feelings for Huxley. 'My loved', she writes to Morrell on 24 January 1917, 'it is not life without you it is not possible without you – just nothing, nothing and I long to be with you and love you for ever and ever.'[25] Since Maria's letters to Huxley (and his to her) were destroyed in the fire that engulfed his Los Angeles home in 1961, it is necessary to rely on Maria's letters to Morrell to gauge her feelings for Huxley. On 1 February 1917, she tepidly declares, 'I care for A so much'. Ten days later, she confides to Morrell that she writes '*friendly letters*' to Huxley, and that, while she is looking forward to his visit, 'he *must be* a friend'.[26] Meanwhile, in June, Maria had become involved with Costanza da Fasola, the daughter of a professor at the University of Florence (who was a friend of Maria's uncle). Maria writes to Morrell of their habit of swimming in the nude and encloses two pictures of them both posing naked in the grounds of the villa at Forte dei Marmi they had to themselves. In a letter to Morrell, who had chided her for toying with Huxley's affections, Maria amusingly expresses her ambivalence: 'I am certain about Aldous – I care for him very much – more now – I think I always did really – only sometimes I care for no-one – and can't bear him.'[27]

After almost injuring his good eye by chopping wood, Huxley had to abandon manual work on the farm, at the very moment when he needed to distract his mind from thoughts of Maria. He made various efforts to obtain alternative employment and ended up at the Air Board in April 1917, which he hated. 'It is too too bloody,' he writes to Julian. 'And then the war becomes more ghastly day by day and every day it becomes more obvious that it is a folly and a crime to go on' (*LAH*, 124). In May, Huxley was required to undergo medical re-examination due to modifications in the Military Service Act of 1916, which repeatedly widened the parameters of those deemed eligible to fight. He was appalled by the parlous state of the men who presented themselves before the recruiters. Later that year he would write a scathing poem about the volunteer army organized by an Oxford don, A. D. Godley, titled the 'Oxford Volunteers' (1917):

Some have piles and some have goitres,
Most of them have Bright's disease,
Uric acid has made them flaccid and one gouty hero
Loiters,
Anchylosed in toes and knees.

'Tis Duty drags their aching carrion
Through the rain and through the mud.
England calls! From Windsor walls sounds
the once Coburgian clarion,
Screaming: Empire, Home and Blood![28]

Huxley's new-found pacifist convictions would also find expression in his novella 'Farcical History of Richard Greenow' (1920). The protagonist is afflicted with a peculiar form of mental hermaphroditism, in which by day he is a high-minded philosopher and communist activist, and by night he is a prolific novelist of cloying romantic fiction whose nom de plume is Pearl Bellairs. The latter's novels are produced via a kind of automatic writing, in that Dick goes to bed and wakes up to discover a new instalment of *Heartsease Fitzroy* on his desk. At the outbreak of war, Pearl takes to writing jingoistic newspaper articles while Richard becomes a conscientious objector. His experience at the South Marylebone Tribunal, at which he is asked by the military representative, 'What would you do if you saw a German violating your sister?', has much in common with Lytton Strachey's hearing, and Richard ends up working on the land at Crome (a fictional version of Garsington) with other conscientious objectors. John Sutherland asserts that 'Miss Bellairs is a hilarious (and transparent) spoof of Mrs Humphry Ward', who was asked by President Roosevelt to write a series of articles to whip up popular support for American intervention in the war, and whose 'subsequent dispatches to the American people are plausibly credited with doing much to bring that country into the European fight'.[29] Even if Mrs Humphry Ward had nothing to do with the conception of Pearl Bellairs, 'Richard Greenow' is an attack on the treatment of conscientious objectors and valorizes Richard's pacifism as opposed to Pearl's nationalism. It is also a vivid dramatization of the mind–body dualism that would inform so much of Huxley's fiction: Dick represents the rational mind, attracted to maths and abstract thinking, while Pearl is the sentimental body or heart, who is attracted to love, religion and patriotism.[30]

In September 1917 Huxley secured a teaching job at Eton. He got on well with the pupils (among them Eric Blair, also known as George Orwell) but pined for good company among the crotchety masters. On Saturdays he travelled to London to see his friends: Carrington, Eliot, Evan Morgan, Naomi Mitchison, Marie Beerbohm and Juliette Baillot (who had been governess to Morrell's daughter at Garsington and who would later marry his brother Julian). His work was being published in small literary magazines, such as *Wheels* and *The Egoist* (which published Eliot, Ezra Pound and James Joyce). A small, privately printed edition of his poems, *Jonah* (1917), appeared in December and Blackwell's published another collection, *The Defeat of Youth* (1918), the following year. He complained that teaching only allowed him the leisure to write poetry but began to work on short stories as well. Although Maria became a more faithful correspondent, with the war showing no signs of ending, Huxley was not sure when he would see her again. Looking back on this period of separation, Maria wondered why Huxley had not thrown her over for some sophisticated Bloomsbury flapper, for she was not artistic or especially intellectual.[31] In the only extant letter to Maria (5 November 1918), Huxley wrote about his admiration for Flaubert and expressed his impatience with the naturalistic, nineteenth-century approach to the novel, with its excessive description both of external details and the characters' psychology. He was then composing 'Farcical History of Richard Greenow' and these formal considerations were evidently exercising his mind.

Come the armistice, Huxley made several unsuccessful efforts to obtain a teaching post at Oxford, since the demobilized members of the teaching faculty at Eton would be returning soon, rendering his services redundant. Moreover, he was anxious to secure a decent income on which he could get married – Maria was currently in Capri with Costanza waiting for a passport to return to Belgium. In March 1919 he was best man at Julian's wedding to Juliette Baillot. After months of putting out feelers to his literary contacts, Huxley obtained an editorial position at the *Athenaeum* (edited by Katherine Mansfield's husband John Middleton Murry) and borrowed some money from his father to rent a studio flat at 18 Hampstead Hill Gardens. In April he was reunited with Maria in Belgium after a separation of more than two years. Maria's grandfather owned a textile business and her father was a partner, but one of their factories had been damaged in the last of the fighting, leaving them financially ruined. Huxley had written longingly to various friends about the prospect of a year off in which to write, and seems to have been expecting that Maria would bring some money to their marriage. Nonetheless, they were married on 10 July 1919 at the town hall in Bellem, Belgium. The only relatives in attendance were Maria's mother and her sister Jeanne.

Aldous and Maria Huxley, *c.* 1930.

Huxley's job at the *Athenaeum* largely consisted of writing book reviews and notices. In order to eke out his income, he also wrote for other publications, such as the *London Mercury*, and was briefly a drama critic for the *Westminster Gazette*. *Limbo*, a collection of short stories and an experimental play, was published in February 1920 by Chatto & Windus and received favourable reviews. Writing in the *TLS*, Virginia Woolf cavilled at Huxley's conventional education (Eton, Oxford), which had resulted in an ostentatious 'cleverness' that left her cold; however, she predicted that 'Mr Huxley's next book will be not only clever, amusing, and well written, but interesting into the bargain'.[32] Huxley's only child, Matthew, was born in April; Maria suffered a near-fatal haemorrhage during labour and was advised against having more children. Another book of poetry, *Leda*, was published in May. In a letter to Juliette, Huxley boasts that the title poem's 'strange mixture of beauty and irony . . . beggar[s] description' (*LAH*, 165). There is a clash of contraries in the poem – divine/mortal, male/female, love/lust, human/animal, beauty/beast, modern/mythic – that was becoming a hallmark of Huxley's early work.[33] But even Huxley's literary friends found themselves hard-pushed to praise his poetry – when asked what he thought of *Leda*, Eliot icily stated: 'I was unable to show any enthusiasm for his verse.'[34]

Though journalism was more congenial than teaching at Eton, Huxley was under enormous pressure to produce enough of it to live on, and in the process was straining his eyes. In October 1920 he left the *Athenaeum* for a better-paid position on the new magazine *House and Garden*. With a new baby and a maid, Huxley decided that the studio in Hampstead was untenable and decided to move to Florence, where the cost of living was substantially less, in order to allow him time to work on a novel. Maria spent the first three months of 1921 with her family in Belgium while Huxley shared the Bloomsbury flat of a friend to save money. In the event, they only stayed in Florence for a couple of months, finding it disagreeably hot and crowded with English expatriates. They moved to Forte dei Marmi on the Tuscan coast, where Huxley settled down to a conducive routine of writing, swimming and reading.

By the middle of August Huxley had completed *Crome Yellow*, which was published in November. For a first novel, it is wonderfully assured, abounding in vitality and charm. Huxley reprises the fictional country house Crome (inspired by the bohemian antics of Garsington Manor) from 'Richard Greenow', though he sets the book in the post-war period. Huxley's protagonist is the fledgling poet Denis Stone, who is besotted with Anne, the glamorous, man-baiting niece of Henry and Priscilla Wimbush, the aristocratic owners of Crome. While Denis longs to be a dashing man of action, he is instead an introspective intellectual who, like so many of Huxley's subsequent heroes, is more at home with ideas and books than he is with real people. Given that his knowledge of the world has been largely acquired through reading, it is perhaps unsurprising that he expects reality to conform to his poetic expectations and much of the novel's comedy derives from the yawning gap between the two. For instance, on his first morning at Crome he plans to tell Anne (whom he has depicted as a 'Hamadryad' in one of his poems) that she looks 'adorable', which he hopes will provoke a coquettish reply, resulting in a 'pregnant silence', but Anne forestalls his compliment by informing him that he looks 'perfectly sweet' in his white flannel trousers, thereby deflating his romantic designs (*CY*, 16–17).

The house guests at Crome view the world through the lens of their own obsessions. When Henry shows his guests the farm, for example, the hedonistic Anne, who spurns responsibility, expresses pity for the sow with fourteen piglets; the Byronic painter Gombauld, whose designs on Anne are decidedly less romantic than those of Denis, exclaims: 'Lots of life: that's what we want. I like pullulation; everything ought to increase and multiply as hard as it can' (CY, 22); this naturally offends Mary Bracegirdle, a virginal exponent of Freud and the sexologist Havelock Ellis, who champions birth control; while the ultra-rational intellectual Mr Scogan predicts the advent of test-tube babies (anticipating Huxley's dystopia *Brave New World*). The idea of being trapped in one's own consciousness, unable to make contact with anyone, is a key theme of the novel. For instance, Denis becomes convinced that Anne has fallen for Gombauld. In the aftermath of the annual fair at Crome, he observes them in the moonlit garden engaged in what he assumes is an 'endlessly passionate embracement', when in fact Anne is emphatically rebuffing Gombauld's advances (CY, 162). After briefly contemplating suicide, Denis decides to cut short his stay at Crome by sending himself a telegram to provide a pretext to return to London. It is only when he announces that he is leaving that he perceives that Anne, having earlier dismissed his strangled declaration of love, has begun to warm to him in light of Gombauld's irksome attentions. The novel ends with Denis bitterly adapting a line from Walter Savage Landor's poem 'Dying Speech of an Old Philosopher': 'It stinks', declares Denis (the word Landor's speaker uses is *sinks*, referring to the 'fire of Life'), 'and I am ready to depart' (CY, 170).

Building on the success of *Limbo*, *Crome Yellow* established Huxley as one of the most brilliant writers of his generation. F. Scott Fitzgerald, writing in the *St Paul Daily News*, considered *Crome Yellow* to be 'the highest point so far attained by Anglo-Saxon sophistication'.[35] Several reviewers detected the influence of Norman Douglas and the country house novels of Thomas Love Peacock. But as with Huxley's poetry, he pushed modern subject matter into traditional forms. For instance, in the character of Mary Bracegirdle, Huxley gently satirizes modern attitudes to sex and art. Mary confides to Anne her fear of the psychological consequences of sexual repression. She has begun to have transparently Freudian dreams that express her sexual frustration, such as 'falling down wells' and 'climbing up ladders' (*CY*, 32). Resolving to divest herself of her virginity, Mary assesses her potential mates at Crome in terms of Darwinian sexual selection, choosing the 'civilized' Denis over Gombauld, whose 'dangerous heredity' (his family come from Marseille) militates against him (*CY*, 34). But when Denis proves unresponsive, she approaches Gombauld, engaging him on the subject of art. 'When I was in Paris this spring I saw a lot of Tschuplitski,' she tells him. 'I admire his work so tremendously. Of course, it's frightfully abstract now – frightfully abstract and frightfully intellectual. He just throws a few oblongs on to his canvas' (*CY*, 58). And when Mary does lose her virginity to the Lothario Ivor Lombard, who rapidly moves onto the next country house party, the 'abolition of her repressions' results in 'a new and hitherto unexperienced misery' (*CY*, 135–6).[36]

The success of *Crome Yellow* was marred by the rupture it caused in Huxley's friendship with Morrell. In her memoirs, Morrell reports that on reading *Crome Yellow* she was 'filled with dismay' that Huxley had caricatured her guests, such as Mark Gertler and Bertrand Russell, and wrote him an indignant letter. In his defence, Huxley replied that the only caricature in *Crome* was 'of myself in extreme youth', and that Denis was the only 'real person' in the book; the other characters were mere 'marionettes'.[37] Bedford asserts that Huxley 'did not so much put "real characters" into his books as use two or three striking aspects of one as a starting point'.[38] That, for instance, Huxley appropriated some of Morrell's traits, such as her eccentric taste in clothes and interior decor, is indisputable; however, it is doubtful whether he intended Priscilla as a malicious caricature in the manner of Lawrence, in whose character Hermione Roddice in *Women in Love* (1920) can be found Morrell's wilful, controlling nature magnified to monstrous dimensions. Moreover, Huxley had no motive for attacking Morrell. In a letter to her from 1917, he describes his stay at Garsington as 'the happiest time in my life', and there's no mistaking the sincerity of their friendship from his correspondence (*SL*, 49). In another letter, he characterizes Garsington as 'a spiritual home' (*SL*, 85). Huxley felt that aristocrats such as Morrell performed a valuable service to the arts: 'The aristocracy', he writes, functions as

> a sort of Red Indian Reservation, where the savages
> of the mind [i.e. unorthodox artists and intellectuals]
> are permitted to live in their own way, untroubled and
> relatively free from persecution. In a little while the
> advancing armies of democracy will sweep across their
> borders and these happy sanctuaries will be no more.[39]

Huxley's sentiments are echoed by Mr Scogan in *Crome Yellow*, who praises the aristocratic tradition of patronage, which provides a valuable bulwark for iconoclasts and artists against the ignorant hostility of the democratic mob. The fact that Scogan articulates views that Huxley held in real life undermines the notion that Scogan is a straightforward caricature of Bertrand Russell; Huxley, like many writers, put himself into all his characters, not just Denis.

2

Dangerous Liaisons, 1921–8

In October 1921 Huxley returned to London and his job at *House and Garden*, having run out of money. He and Maria rented a maisonette at 155 Westbourne Terrace. He was also music critic for the *Westminster Gazette*, but still found time to write the short stories collected in *Mortal Coils*, published the following year. He spent August and some of September 1922 at Forte dei Marmi. On his return, he developed an unmanning obsession with Nancy Cunard, a minor poet and legendary It girl.

They first met in 1917. Like Huxley, Cunard had contributed poems to the Sitwells' anthology *Wheels*, and frequented the bohemian Eiffel Tower restaurant and the Café Royal. Cunard was attracted to strong, brutish men and was thus disdainful of Huxley's sensitivity, though she evidently found him an entertaining companion and encouraged him to tag along to parties and nightclubs. Eventually Cunard submitted to Huxley's advances. She cruelly likened the experience to 'being crawled over by slugs', and dropped Huxley a few days later.[1] For his part, Huxley was still bewitched by Cunard, in spite of the mounting hatred he felt for her. During this period, Cunard was involved with several other men, including the painter Álvaro 'Chile' Guevara, Wyndham Lewis and Michael Arlen (who based the heroine of his best-selling novel *The Green Hat* on Cunard).

At the same time, Huxley was also unsuccessfully pursuing the Bloomsbury socialite Mary Hutchinson. She wrote occasional

Nancy Cunard, 1932.

journalism under the pseudonym Polly Flinders, was the wife of the barrister St John Hutchinson and was engaged in a long-term affair with Clive Bell (the husband of the artist Vanessa Bell). Hutchinson had a 'teasingly affectionate, semi-erotic friendship' with Virginia Woolf, who apparently drew on her for the characters of Clarissa Dalloway, Jinny in *The Waves* and Celia Pargiter in *The Years*.[2] Much of the early correspondence with her consists of Huxley proposing lunches, concerts and plays, and Hutchinson declining. On 28 December 1922 Huxley sent her a telegram apologizing for 'a stupidity that was rather offensive', perhaps an unwanted pass, though it is impossible to know what happened. Hutchinson must have known all about his unrequited passion for Cunard, and would therefore have been loath to serve as a substitute. In addition, she was more interested in Maria: 'Of the two Huxleys,' she writes, 'Maria was the one I loved. Aldous was gentle, aloof, affectionate and even ardent sometimes, but it was Maria who attracted and charmed me.'[3]

In January 1923 Huxley moved house again, to 44 Princess Gardens in Kensington. Wanting to get out from under the yoke of journalism, he signed a punishing contract with Chatto & Windus that required him to produce two new books of fiction a year for the next three years, in return for £500 a year, which would enable him to live in Italy and write full time. Meanwhile, Huxley's obsession with Cunard showed no sign of abating, and in May or June Maria gave him an ultimatum: either accompany her to Forte dei Marmi or live without her in London. Huxley meekly chose the former, and wrote *Antic Hay* from June to July 1923. He drew on his experience with Cunard for the character of Myra Viveash. At the start of the novel, Theodore Gumbril Jr is a schoolmaster who abruptly decides to quit his job and market his idea, born of sitting on the hard oak pews of the chapel, for pneumatic trousers with an inflatable air cushion in the seat. Back in London, Gumbril is reunited with his bohemian friends: the cynical aesthete Mercaptan, the would-be Renaissance man Lypiatt, Shearwater the physiologist and the devoutly blasphemous Coleman. He also runs into Myra Viveash. 'Spectrally, a dim, haunting ghost,' Gumbril recalls,

> he had hung about her; dumbly, dumbly imploring,
> appealing. 'The weak, silent man,' she used to call him. And
> once for two or three days, out of pity, out of affection, out
> of a mere desire, perhaps, to lay the tiresome ghost, she
> had given him what his mournful silence implored – only
> to take it back, almost as soon as accorded. (*AH*, 69)

But Myra is herself a ghost: her voice is described as being 'always on the point of expiring, as though each word were the last, uttered faintly and breakingly from a death-bed' (*AH*, 58). Ever since the death of her lover Tony Lamb in the First World War, Myra has been condemned to a living death. In spite of her promiscuity, she has been unable to feel affection, much less love, for anyone: 'She had tried,' the narrator notes, 'it revolted her now to think how often she had tried; she had tried to like someone, any one, as much as Tony. She had tried to recapture, to re-evoke, to revivify. And there had never been anything, really, but a disgust' (*AH*, 163).

After his bruising affair with Myra, Gumbril resolves to become a libertine like his friend Coleman, who has recently grown a goatee that he refers to as a 'beaver'. During the 1920s there was a game, scored like tennis, which consisted in shouting 'beaver' whenever a bearded man was sighted. Coleman informs Gumbril that his beard has become a means of seduction, for whenever a young woman shouts 'beaver' he uses it as an excuse to chat her up. Inspired by Coleman, Gumbril buys a false beard and uses it to cultivate a new, more virile persona. With his new beaver spirit-gummed to his face, Gumbril undergoes a transformation from 'the Mild and Melancholy one' into the 'Complete Man', a 'massive Rabelaisian' figure, 'broad and powerful and exuberant with vitality and hair' (*AH*, 94). Sporting his beaver, a greatcoat to lend extra breadth to his shoulders and a heavy Malacca cane, the Complete Man sallies forth in search of carnal quarry. Unbeknown to Gumbril, he picks up Shearwater's wife while she is window-shopping in Bayswater. Rosie Shearwater, dissatisfied with her neglectful husband, is also in search of adventure, and is cultivating a new persona of her own, the 'fastidious lady', a shrewd, sexually emancipated patron of the arts.

Spurred on by his success with Rosie, the Complete Man picks up another young woman, named Emily, at the National Gallery. But unlike Rosie, who pretends to be a sexual sophisticate, Emily is a virgin. Hence Gumbril abandons his beaver (claiming to have

shaved), and reverts to his 'Mild and Melancholy' self in front
of her, which is more congenial to Emily's innocent nature. He
confides to Emily his intimations of the 'crystal quiet' that lies
behind the uproar of contemporary life – the 'bandstands and
factories', the 'jazz bands, the music-hall songs, the boys shouting
the news' (*AH*, 145). In the previous chapter, I noted that mystical
experience involves the transcendence of the ego, or, put slightly
differently, the recognition that the isolated ego is an illusion
and that what's real, what one identifies with, is the godhead or
One. Gumbril seems dimly to sense this all-encompassing One
(symbolized by the 'crystal quiet') in nature, and correctly perceives
that the hurly-burly of the capital is an insuperable obstacle to the
spiritual life. In London, Gumbril is embroiled in sexual adventures
as the Complete Man; he makes a deal with a venture capitalist
to market his pneumatic trousers and he spends his nights in the
disreputable company of Coleman and Mercaptan. Thus when
Emily rents a cottage in Sussex for the summer, Gumbril leaps
at the opportunity of sloughing off his base urban self. But as he
hurries to catch his train from Charing Cross, he bumps into Myra
Viveash, who persuades him to postpone his trip in order to have
lunch with her. Throughout the novel, Gumbril has been struggling
with the two sides of his self: on the one hand, there is the Mild
and Melancholy one, who exults in nature, apprehends divinity in
Mozart's G minor Quintet, and believes in romantic love; on the
other, there is the Complete Man, who subscribes to the death of
God, scoffs at romantic ideals and pursues dangerous liaisons. The
longer Gumbril remains in London, the more he succumbs to the
ambient corruption. After his boozy lunch with Myra, he sends
Emily a telegram in which he claims to have had an accident.

That evening, Gumbril and Myra attend a cabaret. The jazz
band's refrain, 'What's he to Hecuba? / Nothing at all', alludes to
the Gonzago play in *Hamlet*, and inspires a nihilistic delirium in
the crowd:

'What's he to Hecuba?' Mrs Viveash murmured the response, almost piously, as though she were worshipping almighty and omnipresent Nil. 'I adore this tune,' she said, 'this divine tune.' It filled up a space, it moved, it jigged, it set things twitching in you, it occupied time, it gave you a sense of being alive. (*AH*, 166)

Coleman is also present at the cabaret, which he likens to 'the first circle of hell', describing Gumbril and Myra as 'two damned souls' to his companion (*AH*, 177). The cabaret, with its raucous jazz band and despairing gaiety, is the antithesis of the 'crystal quiet' Gumbril had hoped to find in the country with Emily. The next day Gumbril receives a letter from Emily, ending their relationship. Heartbroken, he resolves to leave the country in order to promote his Patent Small-Clothes abroad. He calls on Myra for a last hurrah before his departure for Paris in the morning. As the evening advances, they stop for refreshment at Gumbril's father's house in Paddington (modelled on the Huxleys' maisonette in Westbourne Terrace). Gumbril Sr is an architect who is forced to make his living by designing modest cottages. In his spare time, he has been building a model based on Sir Christopher Wren's plans for rebuilding London after the Great Fire: 'Wren offered them', he says, referring to the citizens of London, 'open spaces and broad streets; he offered them sunlight and air and cleanliness; he offered them beauty, order and grandeur' (*AH*, 134). But Wren's plans were rejected in favour of the 'old intricate squalor'; the people, Gumbril Sr asserts, 'preferred the wretched human scale . . . of the sickly body' as opposed to the majesty 'of the mind' (*AH*, 134).

In *Antic Hay* the beauty, order and proportion of Wren's vision stands as a reproach to the ugliness and chaos of post-war London. The neon advertisements in Piccadilly Circus, which Gumbril and Myra repeatedly pass in their 'Last Ride Together' (alluding to the poem by Robert Browning), serve as a metonym of the capital. 'These things are the epileptic symbol of all that's most bestial and idiotic in contemporary life,' Gumbril tells Myra, who professes to adore them (*AH*, 227). The antic hay of the title is a metaphor for the mundane distractions – neon lights, alcohol, art, sexual intrigues and so forth – that prevent the characters from realizing the 'crystal quiet' that lies behind the charivari of London, with its jazz bands, music halls and cabarets. In the wake of the Great War, London has become an inferno, devoid of morality, religion and love.[4]

While Huxley was evidently deploring this state of affairs, many of the book's critics imagined that he was in fact advocating the sexy nihilism embodied by Myra Viveash, who proclaims towards the end of the novel, 'To-morrow . . . will be as awful as to-day' (*AH*, 249). James Douglas in his review of the book ('Ordure and Blasphemy') in the *Sunday Express* balefully predicted that 'if *Antic Hay* escapes uncastigated and unpilloried the effect upon English fiction will be disastrous.'[5] Another critic of the novel was Huxley's father, who found it distasteful. In his defence, Huxley wrote that the book was

> written by a member of what I may call the war-generation
> for others of his kind; and that it is intended to reflect –
> fantastically, of course, but none the less faithfully – the
> life and opinions of an age which has seen the violent
> disruption of almost all the standards, conventions and
> values current in the previous epoch. (*LAH*, 224)

The novel found a receptive audience in what Huxley called the 'war-generation', or what Gertrude Stein would later term the 'lost generation', and sold 5,000 copies in its first year (twice as many as *Crome Yellow*).

In August 1923 Huxley moved to Castel a Montici in Florence, a spacious villa with six bedrooms that Maria had stayed in with her mother and sisters during the war. This would be the Huxleys' home for almost two years. Maria had driving lessons and passed her test in Italy, and the Huxleys bought a Citroën that Maria drove at great speed around the country, visiting Rome in November. Back in Florence, Huxley resumed work on the short stories that would be published in *Little Mexican* in May 1924. In the novella 'Uncle Spencer', the narrator states that in his youth he was a complacent materialist who would have poured scorn on his uncle's mystical beliefs, whereas now that 'it is possible – it is, indeed, almost necessary – for a man of science to be also a mystic' it is his quondam materialism that appears 'rather queer'.[6] Hitherto, Huxley's interest in mysticism had been counterbalanced by his faith in scientific materialism, and this dichotomy had produced in several of his characters a mind–body split, such as that between the rational, agnostic Richard Greenow and the romantic, religious Pearl Bellairs (under her influence, Richard takes to mortifying his body through fasting and self-flagellation). Likewise, Gumbril intuits a mystical 'crystal quiet' undergirding the phenomenal world, but he cannot justify this rationally and is not ready to renounce the antic hay of urban life, 'to begin living arduously in the quiet, arduously in some strange, unheard-of-manner' (*AH*, 146). But around this time, and as a result of his friendship with the science writer J.W.N. Sullivan, with whom he had worked at the *Athenaeum*, and who spent four months as the Huxleys' guest at Castel a Montici, he began to believe that science and mysticism might not be incompatible after all.

Sullivan's journalism on the 'new physics' (comprising relativity theory and quantum mechanics) was influenced by Arthur Eddington, the Plumian Chair of Astronomy at the University of Cambridge, whose observations of the solar eclipse in May 1919 had helped to confirm Einstein's theory of general relativity. Sullivan argued that relativity theory seemed to endorse the idealist world-view that had been gaining ground in philosophy under the impetus of Immanuel Kant in the eighteenth century. Just as Copernicus realized that the planets of the solar system didn't revolve around Earth but around the Sun, so Kant effected a Copernican revolution in epistemology by shifting the emphasis away from the object and onto the perceiving subject. Kant held that it was impossible to apprehend the object or thing itself (the noumenon), in other words as God would perceive it, with total objectivity; all we could know was how the object *appeared* to us, in the form of sense perceptions. According to the two-worlds interpretation of Kant's transcendental idealism, there is a noumenal world of things in themselves and a phenomenal world of appearances or mental representations based on sensory data transmitted from the noumenal world. Kant declared that space and time were a priori forms that did not exist in themselves, but rather served to structure our phenomenal experience. Likewise, in the new physics, the Newtonian conception of a separate, uniform space and time were shown to be convenient fictions. In its place, Einstein posited a four-dimensional space–time continuum, which was relative with respect to the observer. This new emphasis on the observer and her frame of reference was akin to Kant's privileging of the subject over the object. 'It is necessary to keep reminding ourselves', affirmed Eddington in the 1927 Gifford Lectures,

> that all knowledge of our environment from which the
> world of physics is constructed, has entered in the form
> of messages transmitted along the nerves to the seat of
> consciousness. Obviously the messages travel in code . . .
> We are acquainted with an external world because its
> fibres run into our consciousness; it is only our own ends
> of the fibres that we know; from those ends we more or
> less successfully reconstruct the rest, as a palaeontologist
> reconstructs an extinct monster from its footprint.[7]

According to Eddington, the physicist's knowledge of the material world was confined to 'pointer readings', for example the mass or momentum of an object; he or she could not know the nature of the object, or in Kantian terms the thing itself. Moreover, these pointer readings from the material world primarily existed in the *mind* of the observer. For the nineteenth-century physicist, there was no doubting the material nature of the world: it was composed of solid atoms resembling minute billiard balls, whereas in the twentieth century Ernest Rutherford had demonstrated that atoms were largely composed of empty space, and its constituent protons and electrons did not behave in a deterministic manner. 'The physical atom', writes Eddington,

> is a schedule of pointer readings. The schedule is, we agree, attached to some unknown background. Why not then attach it to something of a spiritual nature of which a prominent characteristic is *thought*. It seems rather silly to prefer to attach it to something of a so-called 'concrete' nature inconsistent with thought, and then to wonder where thought comes from.[8]

In other words, instead of getting bogged down in the Cartesian debate about the incommensurability of body and mind, why not posit matter (whose atomic foundation had turned out to be so fugitive and flimsy) as mind. This led Eddington to proclaim:

> the stuff of the world is mind-stuff . . . The mind-stuff of the world is, of course, something more general than our individual conscious minds; but we may think of its nature as not altogether foreign to the feelings in our consciousness. The realistic matter and fields of force of former physical theory are altogether irrelevant – except in so far as the mind-stuff has itself spun these imaginings.[9]

Eddington's position, then, goes beyond the epistemological idealism of Kant (for whom our *knowledge* of the world was ideal, derived from phenomenal sense perceptions, rather than the thing or world itself) and is more akin to Bishop Berkeley's ontological idealism (the world exists as ideas in the mind of humans and God). Eddington even posits a 'universal Mind or Logos' to stand in for Berkeley's God and reify the remainder of the universe not perceived by human beings (though Eddington doesn't quite put it like that).[10]

Eddington's idealist reading of the new physics dovetailed well with mysticism, since one of the most common characteristics of mystical experience is a sense of oneness with God, or with the world as an emanation of God. As a result, many mystics conceived of the universe monistically and regarded human beings, the world and the godhead as spiritual rather than physical entities (whereas dualistic religions, such as Christianity, insisted on the distinction between body and soul, human and divine, and so on).

Under Sullivan's influence, the idealist reading of the new physics found its way into Huxley's next novel, *Those Barren Leaves* (1925). The novel is set in and around the Tuscan villa of Lilian Aldwinkle, another eccentric chatelaine in the mould of Priscilla Wimbush. Like *Crome Yellow, Those Barren Leaves* is a Peacockian country house novel, peopled with writers (Mary Thriplow), literary men (Chelifer), hedonists (Cardan) and aristocrats (Lord Hovenden). Calamy, the protagonist, is the first of a new character type for Huxley: the spiritual seeker. He longs to plumb the depths of mystery, to lift the veil of Isis and apprehend ultimate reality, but he senses that in order to achieve this he must renounce the life of easy hedonism he has been leading. At the end of the novel, he retreats to a cottage in the Apuan Alps, where he can live simply, aloof from bodily appetites, and devote himself to meditation. There he is visited by Cardan, a devout materialist who at the age of 65 is beset with intimations of mortality; he tells Calamy that the spirit, far from being immortal, is in fact the prisoner of the body, and that it will die when the body dies. 'The fundamental question is this,' Calamy replies:

Can you talk of the soul being at the mercy of the body, can you give any kind of an explanation of mind in terms of matter? When you reflect that it's the human mind that has invented space, time and matter, picking them out of reality in a quite arbitrary fashion – can you attempt to explain a thing in terms of something it has invented itself? That's the fundamental question. (*TBL*, 310)

Vanessa Bell, *Mrs St John Hutchinson*, 1915, oil paint on board.

For all his Epicureanism, Cardan seems to be *au courant* with the new physics, for he concedes that 'scientifically speaking, matter may not be matter, *really*.' However, he propounds the common-sense view that

> something having all the properties we have always attributed to matter is perpetually getting in our way, and that our minds do, in point of fact, fall under the dominion of certain bits of this matter, known as our bodies, changing as they change and keeping pace with their decay. (*TBL*, 310)

But that is merely how, Calamy responds, matter appears to us. By practising austerities, the mystics of the past were able to transcend their 'bodily limitations' and achieve a state of mystical oneness, in which they perceived that the phenomenal world of diversity (ostensibly composed of discrete material objects) was in fact a 'cosmic illusion' (*TBL*, 310). It is this ultimate reality, in which everything is the One, that Calamy is hoping to apprehend.

Those Barren Leaves was published in January 1925, by which time Huxley seems to have grown dissatisfied with the book, judging it to be 'jejune and shallow and off the point' (*LAH*, 242). It lacks the comedy and charm of *Crome Yellow*, and Calamy's interest in mysticism and idealism seems a little academic; it is hard to credit that his meditations in the Apuan Alps will afford him the mystical breakthrough he desires. From March to April, Huxley and Maria took a trip to Tunisia, which he would write about in his travel book *Along the Road* (1925). At some point Chatto seem to have accepted non-fiction books from Huxley (the original contract had stipulated two books of fiction per year), as in 1923 they published his first collection of essays, *On the Margin*, most of which had first appeared in the *Athenaeum*. In June 1925 Huxley vacated Castel a Montici, having become disenchanted with Florence, which he described as 'a third-rate provincial town, colonized by English sodomites and middle-aged Lesbians' (*LAH*, 246).

Back in London in July, Huxley finally slept with Mary Hutchinson after a long, slightly wheedling campaign of amorous attrition. It's hard to see, from the ugly portrait of her by Vanessa Bell, what so captivated Huxley: Hutchinson looks like a shifty goose, with an improbable helmet of human hair; Bell painted it shortly after Hutchinson had begun an affair with her husband, and remarked with satisfaction that the portrait was 'perfectly hideous . . . and yet quite recognizable'.[11] There's a more elegant charcoal sketch of her by Matisse (*Portrait of Mary Hutchinson*); she also sat for Duncan Grant and Henry Tonks, and was the model for Erato in Boris Anrep's mosaic *The Awakening of the Muses* in the entrance of the National Gallery. Reminiscing on their liaison in a letter, what excites Huxley is the memory of Hutchinson with her hair tied up in a pigtail making it seem like 'a *détournement de mineure*', in other words statutory rape (*SL*, 141). Maria was in Belgium at this time visiting relatives, but an assignation was made for the three of them the following month at a hotel in Paris, where it seems Maria become physically intimate with Hutchinson, too. In a letter from March 1926, Maria, musing on this period, writes to Hutchinson: 'There is so much that keeps us bound – all pleasure and a great tenderness – think of our amusements – all three together last summer . . . constantly we talk of you.'[12]

In September Huxley and Maria left their son Matthew with his grandmother in Belgium and embarked on a round-the-world trip, which would serve as the basis for his next travel book, *Jesting Pilate* (1926). The first stop was Bombay (now Mumbai), whence they travelled by train to Srinagar, Kashmir, where Huxley settled down to do some writing in a bungalow overlooking a valley of poplars. In December they were on the move again, taking in Lahore and Indore. At Kanpur, they attended the All India Congress, sitting amid some 7,000 delegates on the floor of a huge tent. Huxley was sympathetic to the Indian desire for independence, judging the English colonials he met to be 'beyond all words repulsive'. In a letter to Lewis Gielgud, he writes: 'We really have no business here. And there is no doubt whatever that we are steadily making the country poorer and poorer' (*LAH*, 261). But while he was impressed by Motilal Nehru and his son at the congress, he found Gandhi 'exceedingly unsympathetic', and described him as possessing 'a low foxy shopkeeper's face', which he deemed 'strange in a saint'. Even stranger, given Gandhi's reputation as a famous ascetic, was the fact that he was 'attended by a young English woman called Miss Slade, who sits by him, adoringly, like a dog, handing him his spectacles, adjusting his loincloth, feeding him when his meals are brought and so on' (*SL*, 160).

Huxley had suggested, in his last novel, that the revelations of the new physics supported a monistic mystical world-view, and thus one might have imagined that his travels through India would have consolidated his interest in mysticism, but the opposite was the case. Indeed, Huxley attributed the poverty of India and her colonial subjugation to the religious fervour of its people, which had reconciled them to a 'lot unworthy of human beings', and opined that with a 'little less spirituality' the 'Indians would now be free – free from foreign dominion and from the tyranny of their own prejudices and traditions' (*JP*, 109). In January 1926 Huxley was in Benares, appalled by the myriad Hindus on the banks of the Ganges who were attempting to 'save the sun' during a solar eclipse. If the energy expended on 'imbecile superstitions' was directed into political activism, he contended, it 'might liberate and transform the country'. He predicted that 'India will never be free until the Hindus and the Moslems are as tepidly enthusiastic about their religion as we are about the Church of England' (*JP*, 129).

After their Indian tour, the Huxleys made their way through Malaysia, Singapore, Java and Manila, where they boarded a ship bound for San Francisco. In America, Huxley discovered that he was a celebrity: 'You have no idea how famous one is,' he writes to Hutchinson. 'It is frightful' (*SL*, 173). It was in America that the first germs of what would become *Brave New World* (1932) took root. Huxley had long predicted that American culture would corrupt and vulgarize its European counterpart. What made him indignant was the democratic levelling that was being perpetrated by American businessmen such as Henry Ford (the ironic deity of *Brave New World*), who regarded artists, scientists and intellectuals as elitist. 'Stupidity, suggestibility and business are held up as supremely precious,' he writes. 'Intelligence, independence and disinterested activity – once admired – are in the process of becoming evil things which ought to be destroyed' (*JP*, 280). The enticingly 'pneumatic' Beta females of *Brave New World* seem to have been inspired by the emancipated women Huxley saw in America. In Los Angeles (which he dubbed the 'city of Dreadful Joy'), he observed the promenading 'flappers', who 'give, as T. S. Eliot has phrased it, a "promise of pneumatic bliss"', but 'not much else, to judge by their faces' (*JP*, 265–7). In a later essay, Huxley upbraided contemporary American women for regarding sex as a recreational activity of no more significance than 'dancing or tennis', just like the citizens of *Brave New World*.[13] Huxley also deplored the brash expressions of American modernity, such as huge automobiles, sentimental movies, jazz music, Wurlitzer organs, pullulating crowds, sky writing and so on, and these would be lampooned in the infantile amusements and hectic consumption of the World State.[14]

Huxley was back in London at the beginning of June 1926, where he eagerly resumed his affair with Hutchinson. Maria had hurried back to Belgium to be with Matthew, who had suffered bronchial problems while they were abroad. In London, Huxley shuttled between the Hampstead house of his uncle John Collier (who was painting his portrait), his club (the Athenaeum) and a studio in

Onslow Mews, South Kensington. At the end of July, when Huxley returned to Italy, Hutchinson terminated the affair. However, she seems to have given Huxley some hope of a renewal of their intimacy in the future, for his letters from Florence and Cortina d'Ampezzo have a flirtatious character and repeatedly allude to the 'Onslow idyll'. But despite Huxley's repeated exhortations to Hutchinson to come and stay with them in their new home in Cortina, she never made the trip.

In the New Year Huxley settled down to write a big ambitious novel, *Point Counter Point* (1928). After writing the first 50,000 words, though, he was beset with technical and creative problems, so he started work on another collection of essays (titled *Proper Studies*) to let his imagination lie fallow and to offset his obligation to Chatto, with whom he had recently signed another six-book, three-year contract. Huxley had renewed his friendship with D. H. Lawrence in October 1926, and the following June Lawrence visited the Huxleys in Forte de Marmi. Unfortunately, the climate and the sea disturbed Lawrence's delicate health – he was slowly dying from tuberculosis – for he suffered a pulmonary haemorrhage shortly afterwards. The Huxleys spent Christmas with Lawrence and his wife Frieda in Florence, then headed to Les Diablerets in Switzerland for January and February 1928, where they were joined by Huxley's brother Julian and his family. At this time, Huxley was struggling to finish *Point Counter Point*, which he worked on in the mornings, while his afternoons were spent 'mildly skiing', as Lawrence disparagingly put it.[15] Maria was extremely fond of Lawrence and volunteered to type up the manuscript of *Lady Chatterley's Lover* (1928) after the typist he had hired had been unable to get past Chapter Five due to the novel's obscenity.[16] During picnics on the mountainside, Lawrence bridled at Aldous and Julian's conversations about evolution, since he derided science in general and Darwin in particular.[17] Nonetheless, Huxley reported 'daily delightful talks' with Lawrence to Hutchinson, and was full of admiration for him: 'Such insight, such wit, such prodigious vitality in spite of his sickness, such humour' (*sL*, 205).

Lawrence was the inspiration for Mark Rampion in *Point Counter Point*, an outspoken intellectual, writer and artist who comes from a working-class family in the Midlands. While Huxley subsequently stated that Lawrence's character was 'incomparably queerer and more complex', he conceded that Rampion was the 'mouthpiece' for some of Lawrence's ideas (*LAH*, 339–40). Rampion castigates Western culture for its emphasis on mind over body, reason over instinct, word over flesh. The Cartesian dualism that runs through Huxley's work is explicitly flagged up in the novel's epigraph by Fulke Greville ('Passion and reason, self-division's cause'). Rampion's philosophy aims for a marriage between body and mind. 'Civilization', he declares,

> is harmony and completeness. Reason, feeling, instinct, the life of the body . . . Barbarism is being lop-sided. You can be a barbarian of the intellect as well as of the body. A barbarian of the soul and the feelings as well as of sensuality. Christianity made us barbarians of the soul, and now science is making us barbarians of the intellect. (*PCP*, 109)

Most of the novel's characters are barbarians of the mind, whose intellectual preoccupations have estranged them from the body, such as the novelist Philip Quarles, who is only really at home with the world of ideas and who is discomfited by human contact, bewildered by other people's emotions. Much the same could be said of his creator, and while Huxley, like Lawrence, was 'incomparably queerer and more complex' than Quarles, there are many similarities between them. At the start of the novel, Quarles and his wife Elinor are in India, having left their son with his grandmother in England. Like Maria, Elinor is adept at talking to people who do not speak Quarles's 'intellectual language of ideas' and interprets their inner emotional life for him (*PCP*, 82). And like Maria, Elinor arranges assignations with other women for Quarles, in the hopes that an affair might shatter his carapace of 'impersonality' and reanimate his atrophied instincts and emotions, thereby making him a more capacious, polymorphous novelist. Quarles's mother says of him as a boy: 'He was too fond of shutting himself up inside his own private silence. But he might have learned to come out more, if that horrible accident hadn't happened. It raised an artificial barrier between him and the rest of the world' (*PCP*, 236). Quarles's injured leg (he was run over by a horse-drawn cart as a child) stands in for Huxley's partial blindness. Like Huxley, Quarles recognizes that he is not a 'congenital novelist' and must write novels of ideas, which, since they feature the intelligentsia, exclude 'all but about .01 per cent of the human race' (*PCP*, 303).

Quarles is planning a novel of ideas that resembles *Point Counter Point*, in which there will be a novelist like Quarles planning a novel of ideas. This sort of literary self-consciousness would eventually become associated with postmodernism, but in the 1920s it was

Huxley with D. H. and Frieda Lawrence.

part and parcel of the formal experimentation that was being pursued by modernist writers such as James Joyce and Virginia Woolf (indeed, one thinks of *Mrs Dalloway* when Quarles says of his prospective novel: 'The whole book could be written about a walk from Piccadilly Circus to Charing Cross'). Huxley was inspired by André Gide's novel *Les faux-monnayeurs* (1925), which he read as he was commencing work on *Point Counter Point*, and which features a novelist named Édouard, who resembles Gide, and who is working on a novel titled *Les faux-monnayeurs*, and whose diary contains musings on aesthetics, character and so on. In *Point Counter Point*, Quarles's notebook serves the same purpose: 'Novels of ideas. The character of each personage must be implied, as far as possible, in the ideas of which he is the mouthpiece. In so far as theories are rationalizations of sentiments, instincts, dispositions of soul, this is feasible' (*PCP*, 303). Quarles's projected novel will mimic the structure of classical music, in which a theme is subject to variations and modulations. 'All you need', Quarles writes, 'is a sufficiency of characters and parallel, contrapuntal plots.' The 'novelist modulates by reduplicating situations and characters. He shows several people falling in love, or dying, or praying in different ways – dissimilars solving the same problem' (*PCP*, 302). This device is adopted in *Point Counter Point*: the three main themes on which Huxley rings his variations are (as in Quarles's example above) love, death and religion.

The theme of love affairs will serve as an example of these variations. Walter Bidlake's affair with the aristocratic siren Lucy Tantamount is reminiscent of Huxley's experience with Cunard. Despite the fact that Lucy, like Cunard, was no great beauty, Walter had 'fallen in love with her . . . insanely, the first time he set eyes on her' (*PCP*, 88). Walter has to grapple with the unmanning paradox of being ensorcelled by a vapid pleasure-seeker he comes to hate. For her part, Lucy appreciates Walter's 'dog-like fidelity' as a stay to her loneliness, but despises his '*whipped* dog' demeanour

(*PCP*, 97). Walter's boss Burlap, the editor of the *Literary World*, is engaged in a pseudo-spiritual seduction of the ageing virgin Beatrice Gilray – Huxley was doubtless drawing on his experience of working at the *Athenaeum* under John Middleton Murry, who apparently considered challenging Huxley to a duel after reading the novel.[18] Walter's sister Elinor is driven by Quarles's emotional costiveness into entertaining an affair with the demonstrative Everard Webley, but, despite admiring him with her mind, her body recoils from physical intimacy. When she resolves to sleep with Webley on principle, to punish Quarles, and in the face of her physical aversion, she receives news that her son is seriously ill, and blames herself when he dies of meningitis. Quarles's pursuit of the pretentious raconteur Molly d'Exergillod ends in a humiliating rebuff, for she is only interested in his mind, while it is Molly's body (her prodigious bust in particular) that Quarles desires. Quarles's father has an affair with his secretary Gladys that ends in ignominy. Lucy is driven by sheer ennui into an endless succession of unfulfilling affairs. Only Rampion is happy in his marriage to Mary (a sort of bouncing British version of the German Frieda), who has taught him to embrace the body and revolt against his mother's spiritualizing Christianity.

The novel marks a shift in Huxley's world-view, from the Eddingtonian idealism of *Those Barren Leaves* to a ludic materialism that celebrates the multiplicity of the phenomenal world. Indeed, another way of approximating musical modulations or counterpoint is for the novelist 'to consider the events of the story in their various aspects – emotional, scientific, economic, religious, metaphysical' and so on, and this is what Huxley intermittently attempts in *Point Counter Point*. For example, the music performed for the guests at Tantamount House is presented in several aspects, such as the scientific (the 'scraping of the anonymous fiddlers had shaken the air in the great hall', which in turn makes Lord Edward's '*membrana tympani*' vibrate, which is translated by his brain into

Bach); the mathematical (in the Badinerie 'Euclidean axioms made holiday with the formulae of elementary statics'); the philosophical (each part is 'always alone' and asserts that 'the world revolves around me' and 'none of [the parts] will listen to the others'); and the metaphysical (the Sarabande is a 'meditation on the beauty . . . goodness' and unity 'of the world') (*PCP*, 29–41). Examples of religion or spirituality are treated satirically or explained in terms of psychology or science. For instance, Huxley skewers the spiritual pretensions of Burlap (who is writing a book on St Francis of Assisi and hypocritically affects indifference to mundane matters such as money and sex), and represents the pseudo-mystical experiences of Walter's mistress Marjorie Carling as resulting from physiological changes that occur in the fourth month of pregnancy. Quarles's friend Spandrell insists that life is meaningless without metaphysical absolutes, such as good and evil, and is driven to commit a series of 'diabolical' acts in order to establish the existence of God, culminating in the murder of Webley. Despite the enormity of the act, Webley's murder proves to be a dispiritingly secular affair: 'God's best joke', Spandrell reflects, 'was not being there. Simply not there. Neither God nor the devil. For if the devil had been there, God would have been there too' (*PCP*, 433). The body is revealed not as the seat of the soul (as in Lawrence's philosophy), nor as the seat of sin (as in Christianity), but as a conglomeration of chemicals: 'a few pounds of carbon, a few quarts of water, some lime, a little phosphorus and sulphur, a pinch of iron and silicon, a handful of mixed salts' (*PCP*, 398–9). The novel ends with the loathsome Burlap in the bath with Beatrice, having worn down her mistrust of men (as a girl she had been groped by an older male relative) through a mixture of bogus spirituality and infantilism. 'And what a romp they had!' the narrator notes. 'The bathroom was drenched with their splashings. Of such is the Kingdom of Heaven' (*PCP*, 444).[19]

3

Intimations of Technocracy, 1928–33

Point Counter Point was published in October 1928 and became a best-seller in Britain and America; it was also translated into several languages and proved popular in Germany and France. Huxley was now being spoken of in the same breath as his modernist peers – Woolf, Joyce, Lawrence and Eliot, among others. The term 'modernist' was first used by Robert Graves and Laura Riding in their book *A Survey of Modernist Poetry* (1927), but was not widely adopted in academic circles until the 1960s. Joyce, for instance, would not have thought of himself as a 'modernist' writer, nor would he have recognized Lawrence as a writer working in the same 'modernist' mode. For Woolf, on the other hand, there *was* a new generation of writers who were attempting to overturn the hackneyed conventions of the Edwardian generation – epitomized by H. G. Wells, John Galsworthy and Arnold Bennett – whom she labelled 'materialists' because of their obsession with the external trappings of their characters (the clothes they wore, the carriages they travelled in, the furniture in their houses), whereas Joyce, Lawrence and implicitly Woolf herself were more interested in their characters' psychology and attempted to represent their consciousness through new techniques. 'Life is not a series of gig-lamps symmetrically arranged,' writes Woolf in the essay 'Modern Fiction', referring to the Edwardians' reliance on regimented plots, genre conventions and so on; 'life is a luminous halo, a semi-transparent envelope surrounding us from the beginning of consciousness to the end.'[1] And it was this that the writer of 'modern fiction' was trying to capture. Huxley was often accused of being a writer of 'modern novels' by his critics, but this was largely because he wrote candidly about sexuality and depicted the amoral antic hay of post-war life. But for Huxley, as can be seen most clearly in *Point Counter Point*, the quiddity of his characters is revealed through the ideas they express in conversation or in their diaries and journals, rather than being represented through interior monologues or streams of consciousness.

In fact, Huxley disliked much modernist writing. He found *Orlando* (1928) 'tiresome' and 'so terribly literary and *fantaisiste* that nothing is left in it at all' (*LAH*, 305), and preferred Graham Greene's first novel *The Man Within* (1929), which was at least rooted in reality, to Woolf's ethereal fictions.[2] He dismissed the strident profanity of *Ulysses* as 'simply the reaction of its author against his medieval catholic education'.[3] The only modernist writer with whom Huxley felt any affinity was Lawrence, who had been forced to bring out a self-published edition of *Lady Chatterley's Lover* after his British and American publishers refused to print an expurgated version of the text. Huxley helped to promote it by sending order forms to his friends. He judged the novel 'fine' and expressed his bewilderment over its censorious reception.

Lawrence's influence can be felt in Huxley's next essay collection, *Do What You Will* (1929). Much like Rampion in *Point Count Point*, Huxley propounded a philosophy of mind–body balance he called 'life worship'. The basic idea was that men and women could somehow contrive to reach an 'equilibrium of balanced excesses' between their warring impulses and drives, between asceticism and indulgence, solitude and gregariousness, intellect and instinct. For the life worshipper, the 'end of life . . . is more life' and the 'purpose of life is to live' rather than to deny one's appetites in a bid for immortality in the afterlife.[4] Despite Huxley's enthusiastic presentation of life worship, there's little evidence to suggest that he attempted to put it into practice in his own life. Like Philip Quarles, Huxley was a barbarian of the intellect, who was unable to counterbalance his mental excesses with intuitive and visceral living. Moreover, at this time Huxley was a humanist, who regarded 'god' as a secular symbol for the life process, whereas Lawrence regarded life as a metaphysical force, and wrote about it with religious awe:

> For man . . . the supreme triumph is to be most vividly, most perfectly alive. Whatever the unborn and the dead may know, they cannot know the beauty, the marvel of being alive in the flesh. The dead may look after the afterwards. But the magnificent here and now of life in the flesh is ours, and ours alone, and ours only for a time.[5]

These paeans to life are made more poignant by the fact that Lawrence was in the valley of the shadow of death when they were written. According to Huxley, though, Lawrence was in denial about his tuberculosis, and refused to seek proper treatment. After a brief stay with the Huxleys in their rented house in Suresnes, on the periphery of Paris, in June 1929, Huxley writes that Lawrence 'doesn't *want* to know how ill he is' and 'hasn't written a line or painted a stroke for the last 3 months' (*LAH*, 313). Lawrence would convince himself that his illness was a matter of geography, and restlessly moved from place to place, expecting the new country or climate to restore his health and, when it didn't, regarding the previous place as a lost paradise. At the end of January 1930 Huxley writes that Lawrence has finally consented to go to a sanatorium in the south of France, which he interprets as a 'bad sign' since 'it means he must be feeling very ill indeed' (*LAH*, 327). The following month, the Huxleys visited Lawrence at Vence and were with him on his deathbed. Huxley writes to Julian that seeing Lawrence was 'most distressing' as he was horribly emaciated, 'such a miserable wreck of himself and suffering so much pain', but that after receiving an injection of morphine he died 'quietly' (*LAH*, 330–31). At the end, Huxley writes in another letter, Lawrence gave the 'impression that he was living by sheer force of will and by nothing else' and concludes that Lawrence was 'the most extraordinary and impressive human being I have ever known' (*LAH*, 332). In the wake of his death, Huxley agreed to edit a collection of Lawrence's letters, which was published in 1932.

In addition to seeing Lawrence, the Huxleys had come to the south of France to look for a new house. Huxley had grown disenchanted with the stupidity and corruption of Mussolini's Italy, and had had an unpleasant encounter in 1925 with four fascist police commissaries, who illegally searched the Castel a Montici for a liberal professor at the University of Florence whom the Huxleys had never even met. Prior to moving to Suresnes in 1928, Huxley had been contemplating settling down in Surrey to be near Matthew's first school, but in the end he felt Paris was close enough and might provide him with some stimulating literary contacts. He reports that James Joyce was 'extraordinarily much pleasanter than *Ulysses* and the *Work in Progress* [i.e. *Finnegan's Wake*] would lead one to expect – tho' I don't like either of those two books any better in consequence' (*SL*, 222). On balance, though, he found the Paris literary scene disconcertingly 'Darwinian', and affirms that the best place to witness 'nature red in tooth and claw' is a 'French literary salon' (*LAH*, 338). Moreover, the weather in Suresnes wasn't much better than in London, and so in April 1930 they purchased a house in Sanary-sur-Mer, which would be their base for the next seven years.

In February 1930 Huxley was back in London to see *This Way to Paradise*, an adaptation of *Point Counter Point* by Campbell Dixon, performed at Daly's Theatre. Although 'the actors were so nervous that they forgot most of their lines and ranted all those they could remember' on the first night, the play ran more smoothly thereafter, and Huxley reported that the final scene, in which Spandrell plays Rampion Beethoven's A minor Quartet while waiting for Webley's British Freeman to arrive and murder him, held the audience 'spellbound' (*LAH*, 328). *This Way to Paradise* ran for less than a month, but it inspired Huxley to write a play of his own, *The World of Light*, which was produced the following year at the Royalty Theatre.

The play reflected Huxley's new interest in spiritualism and psychical research. At Oxford in 1915 Huxley had witnessed the telepathic ability of the classicist Gilbert Murray. While Murray was out of the room, his daughter Rosalind would think of a scene from a book he had never read and share it with those present, after which Murray would be summoned, and, holding Rosalind's hand, would attempt to describe the scene. After telepathically describing scenes from the novels *Victory* and *Sinister Street* with Rosalind, Murray attempted the same thing with Huxley, who envisaged the master of Balliol College listening to an essay on *The Egoist* by George Meredith. Murray 'stood holding my hand for about half a minute', Huxley writes, 'then began to laugh and said "Oh of course, it's the old Master of Balliol being embarrassed. I'm not clear what about, but I think it's a conversation about a new poet."' Huxley judged this 'close enough for a first attempt with an unfamiliar mind' and describes Murray's telepathic faculty as 'a wonderful gift to possess' (*LAH*, 86–7). At the time, Murray was president of the Society for Psychical Research (SPR), which had been established in 1882 to study paranormal phenomena in a scientific manner. In his essay collection *Music at Night* (1931), Huxley discussed another SPR member, the philosopher C. D. Broad, and his notion of the post-mortem survival of a 'psychic factor', which, in conjunction with the mind of a medium, enables the medium to access the memories of the dead person. 'The dead', writes Huxley, 'survive, but only fragmentarily, feebly, as mere wisps of floating memories.'[6] The seriousness with which Huxley treated the subject marked a change of attitude from the broad-brush satire he had brought to bear on the occult in *Crome Yellow*. One of Priscilla's guests, Mr Barbecue-Smith, produces his books of spiritual platitudes via automatic writing. At the annual fair, Scogan dresses up as a witch called 'Sesostris, the Sorceress of Ecbatana', and terrifies the villagers with dire prophecies. Moreover, through his brother Julian (who became a member of the SPR in 1927), Huxley was involved in investigating the medium Rudi Schneider in 1932.[7]

The World of Light features a medium named Mr Capes. Hugo Wenham, the play's protagonist, is a philosophy don at Cambridge. Although Hugo's health and spirit are being undermined by his stultifying job as an academic, he is unwilling to relinquish it. Likewise, despite Hugo's aversion to the timid, conventional Enid, he is mindful that he lacks the good looks of his friend Bill Hamblin, and feels duty-bound to marry her. When Hamblin proposes a trip to Guiana, Hugo uses it as an excuse to postpone his marriage. Two months later, Mr Wenham, Hugo's father, receives a communication from the medium Hubert Capes that his son has been killed in a plane crash off the coast of Haiti. After the incident is confirmed by a telegram from the British consul, Mr Wenham continues to communicate with his son at a series of seances and eventually publishes a best-selling book of their spiritualist exchanges. He is therefore mortified when Hugo reappears alive and well. After Hugo reads his father's book, however, he affirms that the information regarding himself is correct and opines that Capes is a clairvoyant rather than a charlatan. Instead of receiving messages from Hugo's spirit (after his death), Capes has been reading Hugo's mind (while alive) by dint of telepathy. Likewise, it was not Hugo's ghost that played the concertina during the seances but 'ectoplasm' produced by Capes.[8] In other words, Hugo explains the phenomena of spiritualism using terms and concepts from psychical research. It was the classicist F.W.H. Myers who coined the term 'telepathy'; Charles Richet (a professor of physiology) was responsible for the concept of 'ectoplasm'; and Mr Wenham's book of mediumistic communications with his son is reminiscent of Sir Oliver Lodge's book *Raymond* (1916), in which Lodge records messages he received from his dead son via a number of different mediums; and all three were prominent members of the SPR.[9] In spite of decent reviews, though, the play had a limited run and, Huxley joked, had 'made less money than any play since the *Agamemnon* of Aeschylus' (*LAH*, 348).

After the disappointment of *The World of Light*, Huxley returned to Sanary in May 1931 and began work on a new novel. As noted in the previous chapter, the seeds of *Brave New World* (1932) were sown on his first trip to America, and since then he had been on the qui vive for signs of the Americanization (that is, dumbing down) of European culture. In an essay from 1927, Huxley argued that the application of industrial techniques, such as standardization and mass production, to the new media (radio, cinema, gramophone records) had resulted in a popular culture devoid of artistic merit.[10] In *Do What You Will*, Huxley recorded his chagrin at seeing the first talking picture, *The Jazz Singer* (1927) starring Al Jolson. Since the halcyon days of playing ragtime on his piano at Balliol, Huxley had developed a towering hatred of jazz, and he finds a 'horrible tang of putrefaction' in the film's music, full of 'yearnings for Mammy of Mine and My Baby, for Dixie and the Land where skies are blue and Dreams come tree-ue'.[11] Indeed, in his untrammelled outrage, he begins to sound a bit like Max Nordau, who had famously argued that the decadent *fin de siècle* culture of Oscar Wilde and Friedrich Nietzsche was symptomatic of widespread racial degeneration. While listening to the 'most penetratingly vulgar mammy-song' that concludes the film, Huxley takes comfort in the 'reflection that a species which has allowed all its instincts and emotions to degenerate and putrefy in such a way must be near either its violent conclusion or its no less violent transformation'.[12]

Huxley may have been gingering up his outrage for comic effect, but the fact remains that he sincerely believed that the population was degenerating. He was but one of many writers and intellectuals in the 1920s and '30s who took an interest in eugenics, including W. B. Yeats, H. G. Wells, George Bernard Shaw, Havelock Ellis and the Fabians Beatrice and Sidney Webb. Huxley's brother Julian was a member of the British Eugenics Society, and later served as both vice-president and president. While Aldous was influenced by his biologist brother, he was independently interested in science, subscribed to specialist periodicals such as *Nature* and was clearly conversant with the work of Thomas Malthus, Charles Darwin and Herbert Spencer. Among affluent eugenicists it was an article of faith, since there was no scientific evidence to support it, that the poor were responsible for dysgenic traits, such as stupidity and turpitude, whereas eugenically desirable traits (intelligence, moral integrity) were the preserve of the middle and upper classes. Hence the revelation by Karl Pearson in 1906 that the working class was out-breeding their social superiors was a source of great consternation in the British Eugenics Society. This phenomenon was known as the 'differential birth rate', and was largely due, Huxley noted, to the fact that while the affluent were shrewd enough to perceive the financial benefits of limiting family size and consequently practised birth control, the poor were too feckless to use contraception. The solution, Huxley believed, lay in encouraging genetically desirable members of the population to have larger families, which was known as 'positive eugenics', and in preventing the genetically disadvantaged from reproducing, which was termed 'negative eugenics'.[13] It should be noted, however, that Huxley never joined the Eugenics Society and expressed reservations about both positive and negative eugenics. For instance, he predicted that the problem with positive eugenics would be that in a society of uniformly intelligent and gifted individuals no one would want to perform the menial work that was traditionally done by the masses, and he worried about the absence of a 'precisely formulated standard of eugenic fitness' in the present, since not only was there no consensus on what exactly constituted eugenically desirable traits, but no one could demonstrate that the ones that were mooted, such as moral integrity and social usefulness, were primarily the product of heredity rather than environment, and only one of them – namely intelligence – was measurable.[14]

Huxley's fears about the differential birth rate, and about the homogenizing effects of mass production, standardization and democracy, reached their apotheosis in *Brave New World*, in which the Bokanovsky Process and Podsnap's Technique produce a myriad identical human beings. The very names are in themselves significant: the former derives from the Russian revolutionary Ivan Vasilevich Bokanovsky.[15] What was happening in the Soviet Union was just as terrifying to Huxley as what was happening in America: in both countries the individuality of industrial workers was being elided as a result of dehumanizing efficiency schemes, such as rationalization, that regarded men as machines. John Podsnap is a character in Charles Dickens's novel *Our Mutual Friend*, who epitomizes the traits of complacency and self-importance, in spite of his mediocrity, and for Huxley Podsnap was eloquent of the bumptious vulgarity of the masses. In light of their names, it is altogether apt that the Bokanovsky Process and Podsnap's Technique should yield 'an average of nearly eleven thousand brothers and sisters in a hundred and fifty batches of identical twins' (*BNW*, 5). In the Bottling Room of the World State, the lower castes are mass-produced in the manner of a Model T Ford: 'Standard men and women; in uniform batches' (*BNW*, 5). As a result of Pavlovian conditioning, each so-called individual is perfectly complacent about her caste, and yet, insofar as they all hold the same caste values and beliefs, such as, in the case of Deltas, a hatred of books and a mania for consumption, they are utterly devoid of individuality. Indeed, in their unrelieved uniformity, and moreover in the sheer quantity in which they are bred, the inhabitants of the World State are more akin to insects than to human beings. The lower castes, in particular, are routinely likened to insects: the 'leaf-green gamma girls' are compared to 'aphids and ants', while the 'black Semi-Morons' are described as 'lice' and 'maggots', a 'nightmare of swarming indistinguishable sameness' (*BNW*, 54, 218, 183–4). One feels that Huxley's authorial revulsion at the teeming lower castes derives, on some level, from his fear that the poor were reproducing with obscene facility like animals or insects in the big-city slums, engendering the next generation of 'mental deficients'.[16]

On the other hand, Huxley was indignant that the masses had had to suffer the mechanization of both their work and their leisure. In the past, the working class had actively to amuse themselves by playing musical instruments, telling stories, staging amateur dramatics and so on, whereas now these amusements had become mechanized and commodified and were passively consumed in the form of gramophone records, radio, pulp fiction and films.[17] In the World State, Huxley takes the mechanization of popular culture to its *reductio ad absurdum*, resulting in the feelies, the scent organ and sexophones on the one hand, and Electro-magnetic golf, Centrifugal Bumble-puppy and Escalator Squash on the other. Since there are no mothers in A.F. 632, Calvin Stopes and his sixteen sexophonists play maudlin songs about the bottle in which they were bred: 'There ain't no Bottle in all the world like that dear little Bottle of mine' (*BNW*, 65). To judge from *Three Weeks in a Helicopter*, the film John the 'Savage' sees with Lenina, featuring a 'gigantic Negro' and a blonde 'Beta-Plus female' (*BNW*, 146), the feelies purvey a high-tech pornography that inculcates the danger of monogamy. The old art forms, such as literature, have been proscribed since, as the World Controller Mustapha Mond puts it, 'You can't consume much if you sit still and read books' (*BNW*, 42). Moreover, the stultifying blandness and moronic happiness of the

World State has rendered high art incomprehensible. You 'can't make tragedies', Mustapha Mond informs the 'Savage',

> without social instability. The world's stable now. People are
> happy; they get what they want, and they never want what
> they can't get. They're well off; they're safe; they're never
> ill; they're not afraid of death; they're blissfully ignorant
> of passion and old age; they're plagued with no mothers
> or fathers; they've got no wives or children, or lovers to
> feel strongly about; they're so conditioned that they can't
> help behaving as they ought to behave. (*BNW*, 193–4)

Thus while the poet in Helmholtz Watson admires the language of *Romeo and Juliet*, he finds the extravagant emotions of the play ridiculous.

Some critics have read *Brave New World* as a significant break with Lawrence,[18] but it vigorously continues his crusade against mechanism, which Huxley had begun in *Point Counter Point*. In the latter, Rampion rails at Henry Ford and Alfred Mond as exponents of Taylorism, mass production and standardization, which had mechanized both work and leisure, promoting a purely mental mode of being that ignores the body and will eventually result, he predicts, in revolution. One of Huxley's stated aims, in writing *Brave New World*, was to satirize the technological utopias of H. G. Wells, and in his letters he disparaged both Wells's personality (judging him 'a rather horrid, vulgar little man') and his work, which he found unreadable, written in a 'dreadful swill-tub style' (*LAH*, 281). For several years, Wells had been vigorously promoting his 'Open Conspiracy' scheme, in which a technocratic elite of scientists and industrialists would somehow (Wells is a little sketchy on the details) usurp the old-fashioned nationalist governments of the world and create a rational, scientific world state.[19] In 1928 Wells summarized his ideas in *The Open Conspiracy: Blue Prints for a World*

Revolution, and Huxley was clearly responding to this treatise in his essay 'The New Salvation' (1929), in which he likens Wells to General Booth (the founder of the Salvation Army), and opines: 'In theory I am all for man living scientifically, creating his own destiny and so forth. But in practice I doubt whether he can. I doubt whether any great scheme of human regeneration, of large-scale social Salvationism, can be carried through.'[20] One of the problems, Huxley noted, is that humans cannot foresee all the effects of their reforms: for instance, machines, while saving time and labour, had decreased creativity and sapped the spirit of the workers. The machine, far from endowing humans with 'supermanhood', had instead rendered them 'submen'.[21]

David Bradshaw has argued that the economic crisis of 1931 led Huxley to call for a Wellsian world state.[22] But while Huxley advocated international cooperation to solve the economic problems of the slump, this is not the same thing as the establishment of a Wellsian 'global government'.[23] Furthermore, it would be absurd to expect the Open Conspiracy to ameliorate the slump when it would take decades for this kind of peaceable pan-national revolution to get off the ground. Bradshaw maintains that *Brave New World*, although originally conceived as a spoof on Wells's novel *Men Like Gods* (1923), ended up endorsing the scientific planning of the World State, with Mustapha Mond 'acting as Huxley's ideological spokesman'.[24] However, it seems to me that Huxley was as sceptical of the 'insanity' of the Wellsian World State as he was of the 'lunacy' of the 'Savage Reservation'.[25] In an essay from 1931, Huxley asserted that both the future and the past functioned as wish-fulfilling utopias that compensated for the desiderata of the present.[26] On the one hand, *Brave New World* can be read as a rebuttal of the retrospective primitive utopia Huxley associated with Lawrence, and on the other it rejects Wells's soulless utopia of the future.[27] If, as Bradshaw maintains, *Brave New World* endorses scientific planning, why did Wells feel betrayed by the book when he read it? Huxley's friend Gerald Heard reported that 'Wells wrote Huxley an angry letter about *Brave New World*, charging him with treason to science.'[28] Moreover, Wells caricatured Huxley in the novel *The Shape of Things to Come* (1933) as the precious aesthete Ariston Theotocopulos, who rails against progress and space exploration.[29] Wells's narrator even refers to Huxley as 'one of the most brilliant of reactionary writers',[30] and the utopian world state forged by the Dictatorship of the Air, with its classless society of scientists and intellectuals, can be seen as a riposte to Huxley, whose position in *Brave New World* is that a society solely composed of superior individuals would rapidly implode. On balance, then, it would seem that Huxley was not quite the 'Wellsian fellow-traveller' that Bradshaw suggests.[31]

In Sanary, Huxley had taken up painting, and after finishing the novel in August 1931 he decompressed by painting still-lives and portraits in oil and gouache. Through Maria, he made contact with some of his famous neighbours, such as Edith Wharton, who lived at Hyères and was particularly impressed by *Brave New World*, calling it a 'tragic indictment of our ghastly age of Fordian culture'.[32] The notorious American author William Seabrook lived nearby. He was an alcoholic and a sadomasochist and boasted that in *The Magic Island* (1929), a non-fiction account of the voodoo cult in Haiti, he had introduced the word 'zombie' to the West. In his latest book, *Jungle Ways* (1931), Seabrook had written about participating in a cannibal cult in West Africa, and claimed to have eaten human flesh, though this was later purchased from a Paris morgue and the meat Seabrook ate in the 'cannibal' rite was actually from a monkey.[33] 'Sanary is full of the usual Lesbian baronesses,' Huxley reports, 'all of them in a flutter of excitement to know Mr Seabrook, because the rumour has gone round the village that he beats his lady friend. One is reminded of the hysterical excitement of cows when they see a bull in the next field coupling with another cow!' (*LAH*, 365).

Also living in Sanary was the young Sybille von Schoenebeck (later Bedford), who was introduced to Huxley through the poet Roy Campbell, a friend of her mother and stepfather, and she soon became a fixture in the Huxley house. Bedford had an intense affair with the German-American artist Eva Herrmann, who had visited Sanary in June 1931 to make a sketch of Huxley for an American magazine. A few years later, Herrmann shared a house not far from Sanary with Bedford, at which point she had a brief dalliance with Huxley. Meanwhile, a few years earlier, Bedford had become Maria's lover.[34] Bedford gives a fascinating account of an average day at Sanary: Huxley would rise late and have breakfast at 10, then work until 1. After sunbathing on the roof of the villa, the Huxleys would go for a swim together in the sea, both wearing straw hats. During the summer, the Huxleys frequently had guests: the literary critic Raymond Mortimer, the writer and music critic Edward Sackville-West, J.W.N. Sullivan, Gerald Heard and others. Lunch would be served indoors by the Huxleys' servant Rina – pasta or risotto followed by fruit, accompanied by carafes of chilled red and white wine. Huxley would devote a couple of hours to painting after lunch and had a studio built for him above the garage. After tea with ginger-nut biscuits, Huxley would settle down to another stint of writing. Before dinner, he would go for a swim or take a walk. He would wear a shirt for dinner and change out of his shorts into trousers. Evenings would end in the garden, with Aldous and Maria reclining in hammocks and listening to music from a gramophone.[35] Bedford also fondly recalled their picnics on the beach at sunset, or atop a cliff, with the elderly Edith Wharton and the poet Paul Valéry, consisting of fried rabbit, courgette flowers and rum punch, followed by games of blind man's buff for Matthew and Sophie (their niece) and sometimes a song from Huxley.[36]

Brave New World was published in February 1932 and sold briskly (13,000 copies in the first year in Britain; 15,000 in America).[37] It was considered so scandalous by the Australian authorities that it was banned, lending the novel a sexy samizdat aura that translated into sales when the ban was lifted in 1937. Huxley's deal with Chatto had become more lucrative and somewhat less arduous: the contract he signed in 1932 gave him £1,250 per annum in return for two novels and three books of stories or non-fiction over three years, and he signed a similar deal with Harper's in America that paid him $7,000 a year.[38] These sums sound trifling now but in today's money they amount to £85,710 and £171,259 respectively; and when added to Huxley's royalties for 1932 (£2,016 or £138,233 in 2018 money) he earnt almost £400,000 that year.[39] In addition, during the late 1920s and early '30s Huxley frequently contributed essays to *Vanity Fair, Harper's, Time and Tide, Nash's Pall Mall Magazine*, and various Hearst publications such as the *New York American* and the *San Francisco Examiner*. In 1932 he also compiled a poetry anthology with comments, *Texts and Pretexts*, and gave the Huxley Memorial Lecture in November on the subject of 'T. H. Huxley as a Man of Letters'.

In November 1932 he began to work on an ambitious new novel – *Eyeless in Gaza* (1936) – that explored the theme of freedom and responsibility. As a feted novelist, Huxley was increasingly being called on to join various organizations, such as the Political and Economic Planning group and the Society for Cultural Relations between the Peoples of the British Commonwealth and the USSR, but he had to balance his social conscience with the exigencies of his literary work. He made a trip to Durham in October 1930 to deliver a lecture to working-class men in Willington on science and poetry, and reported on the distressing poverty and unemployment he witnessed there in an essay for *Nash's Pall Mall Magazine*, which was published the following year. He characterized Durham as a 'city of the dead', crowded with the silent depressed 'ghosts' of the unemployed coal miners and recommended some form of national planning in order to pull Britain out of the economic slump.[40] In private, however, Huxley reflected on his experiences at Durham:

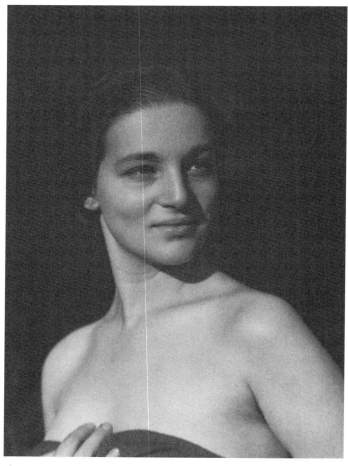

The German-American artist Eva Herrmann in 1926.

The sad and humiliating conclusion is forced on one that the only thing to do is flee and hide. Nothing one can do is any good and the doing is liable to infect one with the disease one is trying to treat. So there's nothing for it but to make one's escape while one can, as long as one can. (*LAH*, 345)

On the other hand, Huxley was beginning to feel that the selfish appreciation of art and the practice of fiction were 'not enough' (*LAH*, 371), but when it came to politics he was as sceptical of communism as he was of fascism. Furthermore, at this stage he was still a humanist who held that 'nothing in our experience points beyond itself to some ultimate reality.'[41]

Huxley also valued his emotional freedom. He had a tendency to hold friends at arm's length, and while always happy to help them financially he had a horror of emotions. Marjorie Worthington, the former wife of William Seabrook, recalled Aldous and Maria driving them to the station at Toulon: Seabrook had decided to return to America in order to cure his alcoholism and was pouring out his troubles to Maria, while Aldous retreated into his intellectual shell and began to hold forth on some unrelated subject with Marjorie.[42] 'I share with you a fear of the responsibilities of relationships,' he writes to a correspondent in 1932, 'have only one that really counts at all, with my wife – nothing else that commits me in any serious way. It's awful to be committed – but at the same time, if one isn't one gets very little in return' (*LAH*, 357).

It's significant that Huxley doesn't mention his son Matthew. By contemporary standards, Huxley was a neglectful father. When he was a baby, Matthew was often looked after by Maria's mother or his German nanny, while his parents travelled abroad. As soon as he was old enough, he was sent to boarding school. There are various references to Matthew's health in the letters (he was a sickly child with weak lungs) and dutiful updates on his growth, but one senses that in the holidays parenting became a bit of a chore, what with the endless 'shopping, zoo-visiting and calling on relations', and Huxley laments that 'there are moments when parenthood is really a whole-time job' (*LAH*, 296). In a letter to his father in 1932, Huxley writes of Matthew: 'Mentally he is the image of M's family', in other words a dullard, 'with a remarkable intuitive power for grasping the essentials of a situation, a natural gift for living;

but with a quite unusual incapacity to grasp and apply general principles – which is rather deplorable if he wants to embrace any of the more learned professions' (*LAH*, 361).

In this respect he was no better than his father, for just as Leonard Huxley put pressure on Aldous (who was less successful than his brothers at Hillside and Eton) to achieve academic distinction, so Aldous expected Matthew not to blot the Huxley escutcheon. In 1932 Matthew was sent to Dartington Hall, a progressive school established in the mid-1920s by Leonard and Dorothy Elmhirst on a large estate near Totnes, Devon. In a letter from the headmaster of Matthew's previous school (Frensham Heights) to his new headmaster at Dartington, Huxley is described as a draconian father who is 'all the time demanding standards from the little chap which he cannot attain'.[43] Huxley was dismayed by Matthew's lack of progress at Dartington, which he felt was altogether too liberal and undisciplined, with too much time spent on pottery and eurhythmics; fearing that Matthew would not be able to pass the Oxford entrance exam and attend Balliol like his father and uncle, he arranged for Matthew to attend the Institut Rauch in Lausanne, Switzerland.[44] In a 1959 letter to Matthew, whose marriage was falling apart, Huxley acknowledged that when Matthew was growing up he had found communication with his family challenging, and was in consequence a 'pretty bad father' (*LAH*, 861). Even with Maria, Huxley could be careless and remote, and he does not seem to have been particularly scrupulous about contraception, for Maria had several abortions that perhaps caused, or at least exacerbated, her anaemia.[45]

Still floundering with the new novel, Huxley embarked on a trip to Latin America with Maria in January 1933. In Guatemala City, Huxley met a man called Roy Fenton, who, like Mark Staithes in *Eyeless in Gaza*, ran a coffee plantation in Mexico. Huxley was eager to see the 'savage' Mexico Lawrence had celebrated in *The Plumed Serpent* (1926) and *Mornings in Mexico* (1927), and persuaded Fenton to take them by mule from Pochutla, a Mexican village on the Pacific coast, to Oaxaca City, a gruelling trip that took them up and down steep mountain paths and through desolate country devoid of shade and water. They broke the journey at Fenton's *finca*, Progreso, 900 metres (3,000 ft) above sea level. There Huxley witnessed the daily grind of the coffee plantations, and in the travel book he wrote on his return to Sanary – *Beyond the Mexique Bay* (1934) – commented on the army of cheap 'sweatable colored labor' required for the European consumer to enjoy her coffee at affordable prices.[46]

In the town of Ejutla, Huxley was accosted by a drunk at the inn where he was staying who insisted on buying him a drink. When Huxley politely declined, the Mexican man pulled out a gun and 'waved it wildly'.[47] Huxley took shelter behind one of the wooden pillars, and finally someone in the bar smashed a chair over the drunk man's arm, causing the gun to go off, but fortunately no one was hurt. While Huxley omitted this episode from *Beyond the Mexique Bay*, he made use of the material in *Eyeless in Gaza*, in which a similar scene plays itself out in Mexico with Anthony Beavis. From Oaxaca City they travelled by train to Mexico City, where they boarded a ship to New York. Just as Huxley's trip to India, far from consolidating his interest in mysticism, had effectively quashed it, so his trip to Mexico terminated his Lawrentian interest in a more instinctive mode of being through the body and the blood, and confirmed him as a self-conscious citizen of the mind. In *Beyond the Mexique Bay*, Huxley describes rereading *The Plumed Serpent* as he travels through Mexico, and concludes that even Lawrence was unable to persuade the reader of the rightness of abandoning the benefits of mind and civilization in favour of submitting or returning, as the heroine does rather squeamishly at the end of the novel, to 'the grand sea of the living blood'.[48]

The Huxleys' stay in New York was cut short by the news that Huxley's father had died of a heart attack at the age of 72. Back in Sanary, Huxley was disgruntled to discover that there had been

an influx of German Jewish émigrés in response to Hitler's rise
to power, including Thomas and Heinrich Mann and 'selected
Hebrews of varying awfulness' (*sl*, 287). Huxley's pejorative use
of the word 'Hebrews' betrays his casual antisemitism, which can
be found in both his novels and his private correspondence. For
instance, in his diary from 1916 he describes Mark Gertler as 'a
nice little Jew-man – with his race's oversmartness'.[49] Nonetheless,
Huxley was sympathetic to the German exiles' situation and in
Beyond the Mexique Bay he deplored the rise of nationalism in
Europe, which he described as a secular religion. Hitler and the
Nazis, by stirring up racial hatred and sanctioning violence and
cruelty, had made of Germany a 'primitive tribe', resulting in 'the
beating, kicking, shooting [and] starving of Jews and Communists
in Germany' with the connivance of the population.[50] Moreover, in
1935 when the German Jew Sybille von Schoenebeck's passport was
on the point of expiring and she was threatened with repatriation,
the Huxleys were instrumental in finding her a homosexual
Englishman to marry (a club attendant called Walter Bedford), and
persuaded a barrister friend of Sybille's to facilitate the marriage.[51]
After the registrar's clerk reported his suspicions that it was a
visa marriage, the licence was withheld and Sybille's passport was
confiscated. The Huxleys enlisted influential contacts and friends
to help her, and when it looked as if Sybille would be deported
in spite of their efforts, Maria passionately petitioned the Home
Secretary, who mercifully authorized the Bedfords' marriage.[52]

4

The Oceanic Feeling, 1933–9

After finishing *Beyond the Mexique Bay*, Huxley went back to work on *Eyeless in Gaza*. But he struggled with the novel's fractured time scheme and was uncertain about the future of his protagonist Anthony Beavis. His original conception for the novel was to show what 'happens to someone who becomes really very free – materially first . . . and then mentally and emotionally' (*LAH*, 376). This is the situation Beavis finds himself in at the start of the novel (dated 30 August 1933), as he looks through old photographs on the occasion of his 42nd birthday in his villa in the south of France: he has a small private income; he has a lover (Helen Ledwidge), from whom he withholds his affections; he has his work as a sociologist to keep him intellectually amused; and his research provides him with a good excuse for shunning human contact. But it still was not clear to Huxley where Beavis would go from there. Despite the languid easy living afforded by Sanary, Huxley missed the London Library and his metropolitan friends. Hitherto, he had made brief trips to London in order to snatch some research and catch up with friends; however, in November 1934 he signed a seven-year lease on a flat in the Albany apartments in Piccadilly, next door to the Royal Academy. He would keep the house in Sanary until 1937 but used Albany as a London base.

It was around this time that Huxley started to suffer from insomnia and depression. There was a history of mental illness in the Huxley family: T. H. Huxley had weathered several episodes of depression; in 1913 Julian had become clinically depressed after a failed relationship with a girl from Prior's Field; the following year, he suffered a relapse and would be dogged by depressive episodes throughout his life; and in 1914 Trevenen suffered a debilitating depression that ended in his suicide.[1] Aldous's depression does not seem to have been so severe, in that he was never hospitalized or attempted suicide, and he actively pursed alternative therapies to help himself. The chief problem seems to have been insomnia, which left him unable to work effectively on his novel. And while Huxley earnt a good income in 1932, in those years when he was not fulfilling his publishing quota he did not receive his annual payment, which meant that he began to worry about money, which exacerbated his insomnia and so on.

During this period Huxley increasingly turned to Gerald Heard, a fellow polymath and writer whom he had met in 1929, for companionship and advice. Heard was best known as a popular science pundit on the BBC, but he also published ambitious books that synthesized history, anthropology, religion, psychical research and psychology, such as *The Ascent of Humanity* (1929). Heard was interested in Indian philosophy and religion, and it's possible that he encouraged Huxley to meditate. Though Huxley had mocked *pranayama* (controlled yoga breathing) in his short story 'The Claxtons' (1930), he now began to practise it himself in order to combat his insomnia.[2] Heard may have also introduced Huxley to F. M. Alexander.[3] The latter began his career as an actor, and developed what became known as the Alexander technique in order to treat the hoarseness and respiratory problems that had beset him while declaiming onstage.[4] Put simply, the technique seeks to improve physical and mental health by achieving conscious control over bad, previously unconscious, habits that lead, for example, to poor posture. In Alexander's case, the bad unconscious habit had been his tendency to tilt his head back while reciting, which depressed his larynx, causing the problems outlined above: by taking conscious control of this habit, he was able to correct his posture and recite his lines with redoubled volume and vigour. The Alexander technique reinforced the holistic *inter*dependence of mind and body, with poor posture exercising psychological effects, while psychological problems manifested themselves in the body. On Alexander's advice, Huxley also sought treatment from Dr J.E.R. McDonagh, who prescribed colonic irrigation and a vegetarian diet. As a result of McDonagh's treatment, the Alexander technique and meditation, Huxley was able to shake off his depression and insomnia by early 1936.[5]

Huxley's embrace of mysticism at around this time was bound up with his pacifist work. In 1934 H.R.L. (Dick) Sheppard, the former dean of Canterbury Cathedral, sent a letter to the press calling for men to send him a postcard to pledge themselves against war, and received 80,000 by the end of the year, including one from Huxley. The Peace Pledge Union (PPU) was not officially formed until May 1936, but it began to crystallize earlier and Sheppard was helped considerably by the input of Huxley and Heard. Although Huxley had been practising meditation and *pranayama*, one senses that it was a last resort to alleviate his depression and insomnia, and that he was far from a convert to yoga, say, or Buddhism. In a letter from September 1935, he writes: 'I wish I could see any remedy for the horrors of human beings except religion or could see any religion that we could all believe in' (*LAH*, 398). By the end of October, however, Huxley had been persuaded by Heard to join Sheppard's pacifist movement; moreover, he now hoped that this would be the tip of a spiritual revival. In a letter to Sheppard on 31 October 1935, Heard reported that Huxley wanted to meet with him to discuss the possibility that Sheppard's organization might become the

point and nucleation of a spiritual movement which may revive religion . . . His new novel is to end with that outlook made clear and as a sort of forerunner of

what your movement will we believe become. He thinks
his novel may be a sort of forecast and prophecy.[6]

The new influences in Huxley's life (Heard, Alexander and
McDonagh) helped him to create the character of James Miller in
Eyeless in Gaza and took the novel in a new direction. In Beavis's
work in progress, *Elements of Sociology*, he asserts that man 'is
simply a succession of states. Good and evil can be predicated only
of states, not of individuals, who in fact don't exist, except as places
where the states occur' (*EG*, 98). This is something that Huxley, too,
had argued in *Texts and Pretexts* and *Do What You Will*, and was part
of his philosophy of life worship.[7] In *Eyeless in Gaza*, though, the
narrative is carefully structured in order to emphasize the long-
term consequences of the characters' actions. For instance, one of
the reasons why Beavis bridles at the bondage of being committed
to a self that is 'consistent and responsible', and embraces the
freedom of being 'a succession of unconditioned, uncommitted
states' (*EG*, 244), is that, at the behest of his lover Mary Amberley,
he seduced the fiancée of his best friend Brian Foxe, which resulted
in Brian's suicide. In the aftermath, Beavis retreats into a cynical
life of detached sensual indulgence and intellectual abstraction.
He is partially awakened from this moral and spiritual slumber
by a freak accident: as he and Helen lie on the roof of his villa
after making love, a dog falls out of a plane and crash-lands on
the roof, spattering both with its blood. This fall is fraught with
religious significance, and is symbolic of the Christian Fall: Helen
later describes the roof as the 'Garden of Eden', into which the dog
violently intrudes, making them self-conscious of their nakedness
and drenching them in blood. Beavis belatedly perceives, while
beholding the weeping, blood-struck Helen, that she is a person
rather than a sexual object, and that he loves her. But he does not
get the opportunity to tell her this, since she flees from his villa in a
state of shock and returns to England.

In the days that follow, Beavis begins to feel he is 'not really there', and that he has been leading a spectral existence ever since Brian's suicide. In this limbo state, he agrees to accompany Mark Staithes on a trip to Mexico to participate in a *coup d'état*. After sailing to Mexico, Beavis and Staithes embark on an arduous journey on mules to the Oaxaca valley, much like the Huxleys' trip in *Beyond the Mexique Bay*; en route, Staithes falls from his mule and injures his leg. This is the second significant fall of the novel, and the next chapter (which is set in 1914) depicts Beavis's discovery of Brian's suicide (who falls to his death from a cliff).[8] The sequence comes full circle, as the fly-infested carcass of the dead dog reminds Beavis of Brian's dead body at the foot of the cliff. When Staithes's leg turns septic, Beavis sets out for the nearest town (a day's journey on mule) in search of a doctor, and presently, as a result of what the narrator describes as a 'miracle', he encounters Miller, who has been engaged in anthropological research and is carrying medical supplies. Miller accompanies Beavis back to the *rancho* and saves Staithes's life by amputating his leg.

Under Miller's tutelage, Beavis undergoes a spiritual rebirth. Miller attributes Beavis's cynical outlook on life to 'chronic intestinal poisoning', and recommends a vegetarian diet (*EG*, 371). He explains the connection between eating meat and petitionary prayer (which emphasizes the ego) and the consequently vengeful religions that approve of both, such as Christianity, Islam and Judaism, whereas Buddhists are vegetarians and practise meditation, in which they try to 'merge their own minds in the universal mind' (*EG*, 373). Inspired by Miller, Beavis joins a pacifist organization and tours England, speaking at peace meetings with Miller and the founder, Rev. Purchas (who was modelled on Sheppard). He begins to write a diary in which he records his struggles to slough off his old cynical intellectual elitism and to embrace instead a mystical monism, in which the universe is conceived as the emanation of an impersonal godhead, thereby rendering human beings divine (since they, too, are an emanation of the godhead). Hitherto Anthony, the intellectual elitist, had tended to regard the masses with contempt; as a corollary of his mystical belief in the unity of humankind, he attempts to 'cultivate the difficult art of loving people' (*EG*, 406). Miller teaches him the Alexander technique, which stresses the importance of the physical means used to achieve various ends (such as speaking, sitting, standing and so on), and Beavis adopts the same ends-and-means approach in his thinking about pacifism. 'Means determine ends', writes Beavis in his diary,

> and must be like the ends proposed. Means intrinsically different from the ends proposed achieve ends like themselves, not like those they were meant to achieve. Violence and war will produce a peace and a social organization having the potentialities of more violence and war . . . Peace and social justice [are] only obtainable by means that are just and pacific. (*EG*, 217)

In addition to Beavis's spiritual journey, there are several other autobiographical elements in the novel. Beavis's mother dies of cancer when he is a child, and his father remarries a much younger woman. With the passing of Leonard Huxley in 1933, Aldous felt liberated to write about his mother's death in fictional form. In *Antic Hay*, on the strength of a passing reference to Theodore Gumbril's mother, who dies when he is a boy of 'creeping and devouring pain' (*AH*, 8), Leonard had accused his son of 'botanizing on [his] mother's grave' (*LAH*, 224). In *Eyeless in Gaza*, not only does Huxley write more directly about his own bereavement, he borrows some of his father's etymological waggery for the character of John Beavis – for instance, Mr Beavis refers to his pencil as his 'teeny weeny penis' as the word derives from the Latin '*Penecillus*: diminutive of *peniculus*: double diminutive of penis' (*EG*, 273). Moreover, he gives a merciless account of Mr Beavis's meretricious grief, which he deliberately works up in transports of self-pity.

Each night, Mr Beavis performs a self-consciously 'sacred' ritual of clasping his dead wife's clothing to his face, breathing in her ghostly fragrance and reading her letters, in order to 'consummate the agony' (*EG*, 132). He refers to Anthony as 'this poor little motherless fellow of mine', ladling on the sentimentality in front of Mrs Foxe, who finds 'something rather distasteful . . . in his words and manner', a 'false note' in the 'expression of the suffering' (*EG*, 69). But for all his ostentatious sorrow, it is not long before Mr Beavis is courting a young woman, whom he marries just over a year after his first wife's death. For Anthony, as perhaps for Huxley, the funeral baked meats did coldly furnish forth the marriage tables. Ronald Clark notes that even as a boy Huxley felt for his father 'a faint distaste'.[9] His cousin Laurence Collier recalled a trip to Rosenlaui in Switzerland, where he observed Leonard Huxley's pompous habit of gazing at mountains and declaiming on the subject of things past. On such occasions, writes Collier, Aldous

> said nothing, but looked at something else or gazed abstractedly into the distance with a fixed and enigmatic smile, and I began to think that he liked neither Switzerland nor his father – a suspicion amply confirmed when I read in *Eyeless in Gaza* the account of the misbehaviour of a goat at an Alpine picnic, an account founded on fact and given with the sardonic relish of a man 'getting his own back' after many years.[10]

The goat in question urinates in front of the Beavis family, who are on holiday in Rosenlaui, whereupon Mr Beavis and his wife start speaking simultaneously of unrelated subjects in a bid to uphold propriety.

After the novel was published, Rosalind Huxley (Leonard's second wife) wrote to protest about the similarities between Mr Beavis and her late husband. In reply, Huxley claimed that Mr Beavis was inspired by the grieving husband in Coventry Patmore's

poem 'Tired Memory', and that his background in philology
was drawn from descriptions of Frieda Lawrence's first husband
Ernest Weekley, whom Lawrence had used for the parson in his
novella *The Virgin and the Gypsy* (1930), though this strikes me as
a bit of a smokescreen. On the other hand, in his letter Huxley
does acknowledge that 'he made use of mannerisms and phrases
some of which were recognizably father's' (*LAH*, 409). Rosalind also
objected to Huxley drawing on his brother Trevenen for his portrait
of Brian Foxe. He replied that he included Trev's stammer and his
puritanical attitude to sex because 'all deeply good characters in
imaginative literature have to be, as it were, diluted with weakness
or eccentricity; for only on such conditions are they comprehensible
by readers and expressible by writers' (*LAH*, 409). This is a cogent
point, and one that Huxley seems to have forgotten, for the saintly
figures of his later fiction, such as Mr Propter in *After Many a
Summer* (1939) and Bruno Rontini in *Time Must Have a Stop* (1944),
seem slightly sketchy and implausible, precisely because they lack a
humanizing flaw.

The ageing socialite Mary Amberley may have been partly
inspired by Mary Hutchinson, for they were both witty, cultivated,
sexually adventurous women. Hutchinson also had a daughter,
Barbara, who married Victor Rothschild in 1933, and Huxley visited
them often in Cambridge,[11] though whether Barbara resembled
Helen Ledwidge (née Amberley) is less certain. When Mary
Amberley's affair with the significantly younger Gerry Watchett
turns to ashes she becomes a morphine addict. This detail suggests
another model for Mary: Sybille Bedford's mother Lisa, who, after
divorcing Bedford's father in 1922, married an Italian architecture
student (Nori Marchesani) some years later, when she was in her
early forties.[12] After she discovered that Nori was cheating on her,
she began taking morphine and rapidly became an addict. At one
point, Huxley gave Bedford money to enable her mother to see a
specialist, and slept with Lisa in the wake of her recovery.[13] In the

long term, despite various treatments and temporary cures, Lisa ended up estranged from her family, living a squalid existence in cheap hotels, much like Mary Amberley; indeed, Bedford felt betrayed that Huxley had clinically depicted this inglorious chapter in her mother's life in *Eyeless in Gaza*.[14] Furthermore, Huxley's second wife Laura Archera recalled that when she met Sybille Bedford, Maria mentioned that Bedford's mother was 'a principal character in one of Aldous's books'.[15]

In his first speech as a public pacifist, in December 1935, at Friends House on the Euston Road (the central offices of the Quakers in Britain), Huxley argued that humanism was uncongenial to pacifism, since advances in science had led many people to reject religion and to worship instead nations and totalitarian leaders. The most propitious 'metaphysical environment for pacifism' was belief in a 'spiritual reality to which all men have access and in which they are united'.[16] At the end of *Eyeless in Gaza*, Beavis uses the same non-denominational language to describe his mystical vision of humanity as individualized waves on the surface of a unifying metaphysical ocean. In thinking of this metaphor, Huxley may have been influenced by Sigmund Freud, who in *Civilization and Its Discontents* (1930) had referred to mysticism as an 'oceanic feeling' of oneness with the world, and which Freud tried to dismiss as a hangover from infancy, since babies have no clear-cut sense of an ego or self that is distinct from the world.[17] When Huxley came to write his manifesto for the PPU, *What Are You Going to Do About It? The Case for Constructive Peace* (1936), he argued that mysticism was part and parcel of pacifism. 'The Constructive Pacifist', he writes,

formulates his belief in some such words as these. The spirit is one and all men are potentially at one in the spirit. Any thought or act which denies the fundamental unity of mankind is wrong and, in a sense, false; any thought or act which affirms it is right and true. It is in the power of every individual to choose whether he shall deny or affirm the unity of mankind in an ultimate spiritual reality.[18]

At first, Huxley threw himself into pacifist work, completing *What Are You Going to Do About It?* in March 1936, editing and largely writing *The Encyclopaedia of Pacifism* (1937), as well as composing anonymous pacifist pamphlets and writing letters to *The Times*.[19] Huxley also gave speeches with Heard at peace rallies across the country, despite his aversion to public speaking. His emphasis on the necessity for 'spiritual exercises' that should be performed by members of the PPU, such as group meditation, met with internal resistance from secular pacifists. Martin Ceadel quotes a disgruntled member from Bradford who complained that the PPU was being co-opted to 'build up a "precious" doctrine which has as its objective the regeneration of the individual rather than the prevention of war'.[20] The point of the spiritual exercises, however, was for the individual to achieve peace on a personal level; only then could one hope for peace on a societal or governmental level. 'Nobody but a fool', writes Huxley,

can suppose that it is possible for a government to behave as a pacifist, when the individuals it represents conduct their private affairs in an essentially militaristic way. Constructive Peace must be first of all a personal ethic, a way of life for individuals; only on that condition will it come to be embodied, permanently and securely, in forms of social and international organization.[21]

Meanwhile, the signatories of the Peace Pledge had plateaued at 118,000 in 1936, which was a far cry from the quarter of a million predicted by Sheppard for the end of 1935.[22] Much of 1936 was for Huxley devoted to peace propaganda, but he found the work boring and repetitive, and felt himself to be an ineffective public speaker. And by 1937 both Huxley and Heard began to feel that the

PPU would never attract the necessary support to make an impact on government policy. Huxley's pacifism also elicited the contempt of several writers and critics, which made him feel out of kilter with the political climate. Cecil Day-Lewis wrote a pamphlet in response to Huxley's PPU manifesto, *We're Not Going to Do Nothing* (1936), in which he derided Huxley's mystical pacifism and asserted that 'we are not at that stage of absolute impotence where there is nothing to be done but while away the time with Mr. Huxley's "spiritual exercises".[23] Furthermore, the reception of *Eyeless in Gaza* was disappointing, with most critics mourning the demise of the sceptical, amusingly cynical Huxley who wrote *Antic Hay* and *Point Counter Point*, and expressing dismay at the mystical pacifist who had taken his place.[24]

When Huxley set sail for America with his family and Heard in April 1937, it was not with the conscious intention of emigrating. Bedford suggests, however, that Maria had a 'premonition' that they would not come back.[25] They cleared out the house at Sanary, and sold or gave away most of their books, including the ones in their flat in Albany. One of Huxley's reasons for going to America was to organize a pacifist lecture tour with Heard and, at the same time, to look at colleges for his son's university education since Maria was anxious to move Matthew out of harm's way lest he be conscripted to fight in another European war. Whether Huxley and Heard planned to return to England or not, they both decided to relinquish an active role in the PPU. In a letter to Sheppard, Heard writes from America that he and Huxley are 'not suited to c[ommi]ttee work or addressing public meetings' and that their contribution to the PPU will henceforth take the form of promoting pacifism in their writing.[26]

After landing in New York, the Huxleys drove south to New Mexico, stopping to inspect various colleges, including Duke University, where the parapsychologist J. B. Rhine had set up a laboratory to investigate what he termed extrasensory perception

(ESP). Rhine tested for ESP with a deck of Zener cards, which consisted of 25 cards of five varieties (circle, square, star, cross, waves), and asked the subject or 'percipient' to guess the sequence of the cards (thus testing for clairvoyance) or to read the mind of an 'agent', who had seen the cards, thereby testing for telepathy. His most successful subjects achieved scores that were significantly above the statistical average of one in five correct guesses.[27] Huxley was fascinated by Rhine's research and in a couple of essays from the period he cites Rhine's book *Extra-sensory Perception* (1934), noting that it 'leaves no doubt as to the reality of telepathy on the one hand and clairvoyance on the other'.[28]

By June, the Huxleys had reached Frieda Lawrence's ranch in San Cristobal, near Taos in New Mexico. Lawrence had been lured to Taos by the American socialite Mabel Dodge Luhan, who had given Frieda Lawrence the ranch in 1924 as a gift,[29] and Lawrence had written lyrically of Taos in his novella *St Mawr* (1925). In a log cabin on the ranch 2,750 metres (9,000 ft) above sea level, Huxley hunkered down to work on his pacifist book, *Ends and Means* (1937), which he had begun prior to leaving England. In the opening chapter, Huxley notes that since before the start of the common era there has been a remarkable consensus among prophets and philosophers on the 'ideal goal of human effort': a civilization that affords 'liberty, peace, justice, and brotherly love'; the disagreements arise on the means required to achieve this utopian end.[30] Huxley's book is presented as a 'practical cookery book of reforms' that can help to achieve these ideals, one built on the dictum of *Eyeless in Gaza* and Huxley's pacifist work, namely that good ends can only be obtained by appropriate means. The chapters on religious practices and beliefs only appear at the end of the book, and for Huxley at this stage mystical knowledge of ultimate reality achieved through meditation was but a *means* to achieve a better, more peaceable society, rather than an end in itself.

In these chapters, Huxley began to draw a bead on the 'highest common factor' in the mystical currents of the Christian, Buddhist, Hindu and Taoist traditions, which he would subsequently term the Perennial Philosophy. The best mystics, Huxley argued, transcend the particular dogmas and deities of their traditions, and make contact with an impersonal godhead, from which they derive their ethics and values, rather than the Bible, say, or the *Bhagavad Gita*, and their teachings are remarkably consistent – the corollary being that the Buddha, Taoist sages and Christian saints all made contact with the same godhead.[31] The other end of the spiritual spectrum, for Huxley, was the devotional worship found in Mahayana Buddhism, Hinduism and above all Christianity, in which the individual seeks special favours from her personal God through petitionary prayer.[32] In an increasingly secular Europe, Huxley argued, this devotional spirit was currently being directed at charismatic dictators, such as Hitler, Mussolini and Stalin, or the deified nations they represented. What united these demagogues was their insistence that ends justified the means, that social justice could be achieved through violent revolution, that peace could be achieved through war, whereas Huxley's contention was that means determined ends, and that violent means could never produce peace or equality, but would inevitably lead to violent retribution, inequality and war.[33]

Huxley had finished *Ends and Means* by September, and spent some time in Hollywood, catching up with the screenwriter Anita Loos and Charlie Chaplin, both of whom he had met on his first trip to America in 1926. 'We even had a glimpse of the ordinarily invisible Garbo,' he writes to Hutchinson, 'looking infinitely ninetyish and perverse, like an Aubrey Beardsley drawing dressed up, for added perversity, in a very sporty Lesbian tailor-made' (*SL*, 349). Huxley had been approached by the book dealer Jake Zeitlin to act as his Hollywood agent: in the autumn, he wrote a scenario called

'Success', and turned down an adaptation of *The Forsyte Saga* because of his disdain for John Galsworthy. Writing screenplays was far from congenial work, as Huxley had nothing but contempt for Hollywood movies, which he maintained lacked subtlety and portrayed a 'crude, immature, childish world' devoid of ideas (*JP*, 199–200).

In October he began his pacifist lecture tour with Heard, but after only a couple of weeks Heard slipped in the snow in Iowa and broke his arm, leaving Huxley to continue the tour by himself. At this stage, Huxley was allergic to public speaking but the presence of Heard had made it more bearable, since they could hold a dialogue onstage; however, with Heard gone (or at least recuperating) Huxley was left to buoy himself by thinking of the money, but even this was small compensation for the tedium of the job. As noted above, one of the spiritual hurdles for Beavis in *Eyeless in Gaza* was to 'cultivate the difficult art of loving people', and Huxley's promiscuous contact with the people who turned out to hear him speak demonstrated that this was something with which he was still struggling. 'I find myself often a bit overwhelmed', he writes to Julian, 'by the curious rigidity and opacity of most human beings. There's something dismally fixed, stony, sclerotic about most of them – a lack of sensibility and awareness and flexibility, which is most depressing' (*LAH*, 428).

Huxley seems to have been planning to return to Europe in the New Year, despite the fact that Matthew was now attending the Fountain Valley School in Colorado Springs. He spent Christmas with Maria and Matthew in Rhinebeck, New York, not far from his friends William and Marjorie Seabrook. In February 1938 one of the Hollywood studios expressed an interest in 'Success', and Huxley decided to head to Los Angeles after he had finished up the last leg of his lecture tour. As it turned out, the studio did not buy his scenario, and Huxley came down with pneumonia and a severe attack of hives in February. He spent three weeks in hospital, suffered a relapse in May and was harried by bronchial problems for the rest of the year. In July Anita Loos persuaded MGM to hire Huxley to write a treatment for a biopic of Marie Curie, starring Greta Garbo, for which he was paid $15,000. This relieved him of much anxiety, as he had been unable to work while ill, and had begun a formidable novel about the nature of narrative which would express 'some kind of general theory of the world' (*LAH*, 437), and would require years to write. In Europe, Huxley had shuttled back and forth between London and Sanary, but Los Angeles combined the advantages of the former (books, libraries, stimulating friends) with the balmy weather of the latter. Another reason for remaining in Los Angeles was that Huxley's sight had been deteriorating – for several years now, Maria had been reading books to Huxley out loud in the evenings to spare his eyes – and he had begun taking lessons in the Bates method of visual re-education. Dr W. H. Bates was a New York oculist who, Huxley writes, 'came to the conclusion that the great majority of visual defects were functional and due to faulty habits of use'.[34] This chimed with the teaching of F. M. Alexander, which inculcated the importance of the physical means used to achieve various ends. In *The Art of Seeing* (1942), Huxley noted that for long-sighted people like himself, the strain involved in trying to focus the eyes impairs the vision, thereby creating a negative feedback loop, with worse vision leading to ever greater strain.[35] This is what Alexander termed 'end-gaining', concentrating solely on the end (better vision) and ignoring the 'means-whereby' that end is to be achieved.[36] A key part of the Bates method was learning to relax the eye and 'to train the mind to interpret what the eye sends it and not to interfere with the functioning of the eye by straining or staring' (*LAH*, 442). As a result of the Bates method, Huxley was able to see without glasses and to read without the fatigue and strain that had afflicted him in the past. In his preface to *The Art of Seeing*, Huxley reports that his 'vision, though very far from normal, is about twice as good as it used to be when I wore spectacles'.[37]

In February 1939 Huxley abandoned his big meta-novel on narrative and language and began a shorter, more manageable book, *After Many a Summer* (1939), set in Los Angeles. The title derives from Tennyson's poem 'Tithonus', the mortal who petitions his divine lover Eos for eternal life but forgets to stipulate eternal youth, and suffers a deathless decrepitude. In the novel, the sixty-year-old magnate Jo Stoyte longs for immortality and employs the unscrupulous scientist Dr Obispo to find an elixir of life. Somewhat improbably, Stoyte is friends with a mystic named Mr Propter, who expounds an incredibly austere philosophy that associates evil with time and good with eternity, in the form of either animal grace (good health) or the mystic's transcendence of personality and experience of the godhead.

Early on in the novel, Propter is depicted in mental prayer, a discursive form of contemplation favoured by Catholic mystics, which begins with a meditation on Scripture, or in Propter's case quotations from Cardinal Bérulle's definition of man ('A nothingness surrounded by God, indigent and capable of God, filled with God if he so desires') and the German mystic John Tauler's definition of God as 'a being withdrawn from creatures, a nothingness capable of free power, filled with a pure working' (*AMAS*, 90). This culminates in an episode of mystical union, in which Propter transcends his personality and the world of time and identifies with God. Huxley rather awkwardly describes Propter's 'awareness' undergoing a transition from being 'intellectual in character' to being

> intuitive and direct, so that the nature of man in his potentiality and of God in actuality were realized by an analogue of sensuous experience, by a kind of unmediated participation.
>   The busy nothingness of his being experienced itself as transcended in the felt capacity for peace and purity, for the withdrawal from revulsion and desires, for the blissful freedom from personality. (*AMAS*, 100)

Huxley with his son Matthew, mid- to late 1930s.

This is what Stace termed 'introvertive experience', a turning away from the world in order to unite with a transcendent God, whereas extrovertive experiences affirm the One in the many, or the godhead in the world. Religions that represent the godhead as immanent in the world are termed life- or world-affirming while those that represent the godhead as transcending the world and human beings are termed life-denying. *After Many a Summer*, given its revulsion for the 'strictly human' world of time, the body, sex, personality and politics, exhibits an unambiguously life-denying attitude.

Jo Stoyte is only the most egregious example of the worldly or unregenerate man who is beleaguered by the 'evils' of time, craving and personality. His obsession with time takes the form of a fear of death. Whenever he gets angry, he repeats the following bromide from the Christian Science of Mary Baker Eddy lest he suffer a second stroke: 'God is love. There is no death' (*AMAS*, 32). Mrs Eddy maintained that the 'real universe' was spiritual, and that the material world and the physical body were illusions, and therefore 'what appears to the senses to be death is but a mortal illusion.'[38] Nevertheless, Stoyte fears the divine judgement described in Hebrews 10:31, the text of which was inscribed over his cot: 'IT IS A TERRIBLE THING TO FALL INTO THE HANDS OF THE LIVING GOD' (*AMAS*, 37). Stoyte is trapped inside his ageing body (pitilessly described as a 'smelly old gut-sack') and tormented by his idolatrous attachment to his 'child-mistress', Virginia Maunciple (Stoyte and Maunciple were inspired by the media magnate William Randolph Hearst and his much younger, ex-chorus girl mistress Marion Davies). Although 22 years old, Virginia looks much younger and has an 'air of being hardly adolescent, of not having reached the age of consent' (*AMAS*, 45). For Stoyte, Virginia's combination of 'the appearance of innocence and the fact of experience' inspires in him feelings of the 'purest father-love and the most violent eroticism' (*AMAS*, 44). Stoyte suspects that Virginia is cheating on him and he winds up mistakenly killing Obispo's assistant Pete Boone in a jealous rage, then has to bribe Obispo (whom he had meant to kill and who actually was sleeping with Virginia) to cover it up.

Pete, who fought on the Republican side in the Spanish Civil War, would seem to be a more upstanding character, but he too is trapped on the human level of time and personality, craving and aversion, and is therefore complicit in the multifarious forms of human evil. For instance, while Pete imagined he was doing good in Spain by fighting for the ideals of democracy and freedom, he was, according to Propter, engaged in a form of narcissism, since ideals are but projections of the ego. Thus Pete's putative self-sacrifice was in reality an intensification of the self, which is evil, given that the goal of human life is mystical knowledge of God through transcendence of the ego. Likewise, even the most idealistic politicians and philanthropists, trapped on the 'strictly human level of time and craving', are unable to 'achieve anything but evil'; the best reforms merely deflect 'evil from old channels into new and slightly different channels' (*AMAS*, 118). Propter's comments are indicative of Huxley's disillusionment with politics. In October 1939 he refused to sign the French writer Roger Caillois's declaration against Hitler: 'I regret that I cannot do this, as I do not feel that politics (except such politics as are dictated by the need to make the world safe for mystical experience) are my affair' (*SL*, 361).

Propter's insistence that 'time is evil' (*AMAS*, 106) is illustrated by the plot. Stoyte and Obispo, in their quest for immortality, track down the Fifth Earl of Gonister, who was born in 1738 and has kept himself alive by consuming raw carp guts. In his mid-nineties, the Fifth Earl held a girl captive in the cellars of his house (Selford) and subjected her to his sadistic 'investigations'; when she escaped and informed the local 'rabble', he was compelled to fake his own death in order to evade punishment, thereafter living in the cellars with his housekeeper, on whom he continued to exercise his sadism. In a network of cellars underneath Selford, Stoyte and Obispo find the Fifth Earl, who is now 201, transmogrified into a 'foetal ape that has had time to grow up' (*AMAS*, 311). This is not so much a regression *from* man to ape as a long-delayed maturation of man *to* ape. The idea behind this is neoteny, which is the 'preservation, in the adult stage, of what were embryonic characters in the ancestor'.[39] The adult human resembles the young or embryonic ape, which has a large head (in relation to its body), flat face and relatively short arms and legs. A mutation occurs, Pete tells Propter, that 'retard[s] the development rate. You grow up; but you do it so slowly that you're dead before you've stopped being like your great-great-grandfather's foetus' (*AMAS*, 102).[40] The Fifth Earl, due to his great age, has had time to develop simian features, such as the 'ridge above the eyes', the 'curious distortions of the lower jaws, the accretions of bone in front of the ears' (*AMAS*, 312). But Stoyte is so desperate for more time that he seems quite willing to submit to the same treatment (and eventually to share the same fate): 'How long do you figure it would take before a person went like that?' he asks Obispo. 'I mean, it wouldn't happen at once.' And, having just witnessed the simian Fifth Earl beating his housekeeper, who has been kept alive on the same diet, Stoyte comments: 'And once you get over the first shock – well, they look like they were having a pretty good time' (*AMAS*, 314).

When *After Many a Summer* was published in October 1939, the Second World War was already under way, and the novel's uncompromising message – either remain on the human level of time, and suffer the slings and arrows of attachment and aversion, or attempt to attain the level of eternity through a life-denying asceticism – was derided by several critics. 'Retreat to mysticism', wrote the reviewer in *Nature*, 'is a poor prescription for the millions who already, through the turn of political fortune, have to face a violent death.'[41] Perhaps the most perceptive criticism came from George Orwell, who complained in a private letter that 'the more holy [Huxley] gets, the more his books stink with sex.'[42] There is, indeed, a promiscuous mingling of the sacred and the sexual in the novel. In Virginia's bedroom there is a shrine to the Virgin Mary as well as Watteau's elegiac celebration of love, *Embarkation for Cythera*. The English scholar Jeremy Pordage is delighted to discover among the Hauberk papers he has been hired to catalogue a copy of the Marquis de Sade's *Les cent-vingt jours de Sodome* in the covers of the Book of Common Prayer. Stoyte's cemetery, the Beverly Pantheon, is filled not with memento mori but with statues of 'exuberantly nubile' women, which collectively represent the victory not of the 'spirit but of the body, the well-fed body, for ever youthful, immortally athletic, indefatigably sexy' (*AMAS*, 11, 14). The director of the Beverly Pantheon pleads with Stoyte for 'just one Early Christian Virgin with her hands tied behind her back – because people got such a kick out of anything to do with ropes or handcuffs' (*AMAS*, 11, 205). If Huxley were merely creating a motif to symbolize the contradictory impulses of the spirit and the flesh, he was over-egging the pudding. In an essay from *Proper Studies* (1927), Huxley noted how, for Jung, the unconscious acts as a balance to the concerns of the conscious mind and thus it follows 'that the consciously convinced puritan is deeply preoccupied in his unconscious mind with precisely those sexual matters which he professes to hate'.[43] This point is exemplified by *After Many a Summer*, which consciously advocates spiritual salvation by abjuring the flesh, but is irrepressibly preoccupied with sex, pornography and sadomasochism. Blake's famous adage about Milton that he was 'of the Devil's party without knowing it' is germane to Huxley here, for his writing really comes alive when depicting sex and sin, for instance in the journal of the sadistic Fifth Earl, whereas Propter's endless moral homilies about the strictly human world of time and suffering emerge as lifeless slabs of exposition.

5

The Perennial Philosophy, 1939–45

One of Huxley's closest friends during the Second World War
was an Indian sage named Jiddu Krishnamurti. During their
first meeting in April 1938, they discovered that they had much in
common: they were both pacifists; they had lost their mothers at
an early age; they were convinced that the nations that were intent
on war were representative of their citizens' aggression, greed and
lust for power, and thus maintained that peace must begin with
the individual. Krishnamurti's house in Ojai, California, became
'a haven for pacifists' during the conflict, much as Garsington
had done during the Great War.[1] Huxley was encouraged by their
company, as he felt guilty for leaving friends and family behind in
England, and his mystical pacifism was increasingly drawing fire
from critics at home.

Krishnamurti had first come to prominence through his
association with the Theosophical Society, which was established
by Helena Blavatsky, Henry Steel Olcott and others in 1875.
The Theosophists believed that all religions originally derived
from an ancient wisdom religion Blavatsky termed the Secret
Doctrine, which could be esoterically glimpsed in sacred texts
beneath the surface or exoteric meaning. Some of the most notable
religious leaders – including Christ, Buddha, Confucius, Moses
and Plato – were adepts of the Secret Doctrine. Every religion,
Blavatsky affirmed, had esoteric and exoteric teachings, the former
being reserved for the initiated and the latter for the masses. In

Buddhism, for example, there is the esoteric Mahayana school and the exoteric 'Hinayana' school.[2] Christ used an esoteric teaching among his disciples ('To you it is given to know the mysteries of the kingdom of heaven'), and employed parables when addressing the exoteric masses.[3] Blavatsky claimed that she had studied the Secret Doctrine in the clandestine Himalayan home of the Master Koot Hoomi. The Masters comprised an occult brotherhood that helped to disseminate the Secret Doctrine and, though human, they had acquired supernormal powers, such as telepathy and the ability to project themselves anywhere in the world (known as astral travel). Blavatsky was instrumental in converting Annie Besant, the former campaigner for birth control and the National Secular Society, to Theosophy. After the deaths of Blavatsky and Olcott, Besant became president of the Theosophical Society in 1907 and worked closely with Charles Leadbeater, who controversially claimed to be an intimate of the Masters. While she was alive, Blavatsky had mediated contact between the Masters and select Theosophists through letters, which often appeared through cracks in the ceiling and in other unorthodox ways, but Leadbeater maintained that the Masters had appeared before him in person and helped him to cultivate clairvoyant powers, which allowed him to communicate with them at will and to access the 'akashic records' (an occult database of everything that has happened in the universe). Under Leadbeater's guidance, Besant also developed clairvoyant powers, and together they investigated the previous incarnations of fellow Theosophists, performed occult analyses of the atom using 'astral sight' and surveyed the mythical continents of Atlantis and Lemuria.[4]

In the spring of 1909 Leadbeater spotted Krishnamurti playing on the beach at the Theosophical HQ in Adyar, India, and was struck by his singular aura. A few days later, Leadbeater consulted the akashic records and discovered that Krishnamurti was part of a prestigious group of 'servers' who, alongside

Besant and Leadbeater, had assisted the Masters Morya and Koot Hoomi down through the ages. Leadbeater announced that Krishnamurti was the vehicle for the coming incarnation of the World Teacher, the Lord Maitreya, and that the Master Koot Hoomi had instructed him to prepare the boy for this purpose.[5] In light of Krishnamurti's new role as the next World Teacher, he was removed from the care of his impecunious father and Besant became his legal guardian.[6] While Leadbeater took charge of his worldly education by day, the Master Koot Hoomi allegedly oversaw his astral apprenticeship at night.[7] In 1911 Krishnamurti came to England in order to obtain a university education, but the World Teacher repeatedly failed the entrance examinations. As a young man, Krishnamurti was extraordinarily handsome, and he was much admired by the rich lady Theosophists he met in London, such as Emily Lutyens (wife of the architect Sir Edwin), who made generous contributions to a fund that had been set up for the messiah.[8] After the First World War Krishnamurti began to speak at Theosophical conventions across Europe and soon attracted a large and enthusiastic following.

In 1922, while staying at Ojai, Krishnamurti made a spiritual breakthrough, though not in the manner the Theosophists had been expecting. On 18 August Krishnamurti had an extrovertive mystical experience, which he reported in a letter to Besant:

> There was a man mending the road; that man was myself; the pickaxe he held was myself; the very stone which he was breaking was a part of me . . . Just then there was a car passing by at some distance; I was the driver, the engine and the tyres; as the car went further away from me, I was going away from myself. I was in everything, or rather everything was in me.[9]

This type of mystical experience had no place in Theosophy. For occultists such as Blavatsky and Leadbeater, there was no need to meditate and transcend the self in mystical union, when they could allegedly communicate with the Masters telepathically or consult the akashic records. The idea, then, that Krishnamurti had had a conventional mystical experience was deeply troubling to Theosophists. Meanwhile, Krishnamurti had grown disillusioned with Leadbeater (who was repeatedly accused, though never convicted, of sexual misconduct with adolescent boys[10]), and his faith in Theosophy was shaken by the death of his brother Nitya in 1925. He dismayed loyal Theosophists by speaking of his union with what he termed the 'Beloved', which seemed much closer to a mystical godhead than were the Lord Maitreya and Koot Hoomi ('My Beloved is the open skies, the flower, every human being').[11] Finally, in 1929, Krishnamurti renounced his role as World Teacher by proclaiming that 'truth is a pathless land', the corollary being that the individual must find truth by herself, without the aid of Masters, messiahs or the Theosophical Society.[12] Since then, Krishnamurti had established himself as a spiritual teacher in his own right and by the time he met Huxley he was attracting devoted audiences in America, Europe, Australia and India.[13]

Another spiritual contact from around this time was Swami Prabhavananda, who was in charge of the Vedanta Society of Southern California. The Vedanta Societies of America are part of the Ramakrishna Mission, an organization that was founded in 1897 by Swami Vivekananda. In the 1893 World Parliament of Religions in Chicago, the dashing, charismatic Vivekananda had won many admirers by proclaiming Hinduism to be a universal religion that recognized all religions as means whereby geographically diverse people from different backgrounds could reach the same goal, what he termed 'God realisation'.[14] On a subsequent trip to the u.s., Vivekananda set up the Vedanta Society of America. Christopher Isherwood, in his introduction to the anthology *Vedanta for the Western World* (1945), affirms that Vedanta can be reduced to three propositions: 'First, that Man's real nature

Jiddu Krishnamurti as a young man.

is divine. Second, that the aim of human life is to realize this divine nature. Third, that all religions are essentially in agreement.'[15] The key teachings of Advaita (non-dual) Vedanta come from the Upanishads. The first and second of Isherwood's tenets are illustrated by the Sanskrit maxim *tat tvam asi* ('you are That').

The phrase occurs in the Chandogya Upanishad, in which Svetaketu, an arrogant student of the Vedas, is taught by his father that *brahman* (the Vedantic godhead) permeates his body like salt dissolved in water: 'That is Reality,' his father informs him. 'That is Truth. THOU ART THAT' (i.e. *brahman*).[16]

This is allied to another key concept inculcated by the Upanishads, and one that Huxley often repeated: that the 'Atman, or immanent eternal Self, is one with Brahman' (*PP*, 2). In the Katha Upanishad, Yama, the god of death, informs Nachiketas: 'Concealed in the heart of all beings is the Atman, the Spirit, the Self; smaller than the smallest atom, greater than the vast spaces. The man who surrenders his human will leaves sorrow behind, and beholds the glory of the Atman by the grace of the Creator.'[17] The 'Creator' is *brahman*: 'There is one Ruler [*brahman*], the Spirit that is in all things, who transforms his own form into many'. Just as 'the wind, though one, takes new forms in whatever it enters, the Spirit, though one, takes new forms in all things that live. He is within all, and is also outside.'[18] *Brahman*, then, both transcends the world and is immanent in it, whereas the Christian God creates the world and thereafter transcends it – He is not immanent in it. As previously noted, Christianity is a dualistic religion, whereas Advaita Vedanta is monistic, since there is no rigid distinction between body and soul, *atman* and *brahman*. In order to realize the divine inside himself (in other words the *atman*), man must 'surrender his human will'. One method of doing this is yoga (yoking or union), which is first mentioned in the Upanishads. In order to achieve union with *brahman*, one must practise yoga, which in this context means meditation. At the end of the Katha Upanishad, Nachiketas, having mastered the 'whole teaching of inner-union, of Yoga', 'reached Brahman' and obtained enlightenment.[19]

Huxley and Heard had made contact with Prabhavananda in 1939 and received formal training in meditation from him. It was through Heard that Isherwood, another English expatriate,

began to study with Prabhavananda. Isherwood had become a
pacifist after his German boyfriend Heinz Neddermeyer was
conscripted into the Nazi army; Isherwood refused to connive
in Heinz's death by fighting for the British, and after moving
to America in 1939, he sought advice from Heard, who was a
prominent pacifist and erstwhile friend.[20] But where Isherwood
soon became Prabhavananda's disciple, lived for some years at the
Vedanta Center at Ivar Avenue in Hollywood and was ordained as
a Ramakrishna monk in 1943, Huxley and Heard were too eclectic
to commit themselves to a single philosophy. Moreover, Isherwood
notes that 'Aldous and Prabhavananda were temperamentally far
apart', for the latter was 'strongly devotional', whereas 'Aldous
was much more akin to his friend Krishnamurti', who, as a former
Hindu and Theosophist, 'was repelled by devotional religion
and its rituals' and 'greatly disapproved of the guru–disciple
relationship'.[21] To illustrate the devotionalism practised under
Prabhavananda, Isherwood describes the shrine at the Ivar
Avenue Vedanta Center, which included images of Ramakrishna
(Vivekananda's guru), Buddha, Christ, Krishna and some lesser
Hindu deities. Huxley felt that worship of a personal god such as
Krishna, rather than the impersonal godhead *brahman*, implied a
dualism between the human and the divine, whereas the thrust of
Advaita Vedanta was that since human beings were permeated by
brahman, they too were divine.

At the time, Huxley was taking lessons in the Bates method
six days a week with Margaret Corbett and had a family to
support – in addition to Matthew and Maria, there were Maria's
mother and her sisters; he was also working on an adaptation of
Pride and Prejudice for MGM, and thus couldn't commit himself
fully to the spiritual life. Gerald Heard, on the other hand, was
homosexual and had no family of his own and was not beholden
to earn a living, having inherited money and land from his former
employer and friend Horace Plunkett (an Anglo-Irish author and

Huxley and Swami Prabhavananda, early 1950s.

Unionist MP). Furthermore, Heard was living with his ex-partner Chris Wood, whose family business in condiments had made him independently wealthy.[22] Heard had the liberty, then, to meditate for six hours a day and eagerly embraced the asceticism of the spiritual path, forswearing meat, fish and alcohol. Heard had also been celibate since the mid-1930s, and prior to that his libido had been primarily channelled into a sartorial fetishism, and thus he had no problem in adhering to the sexual abstinence required for spiritual progress.[23] In his memoir of this period, *My Guru and His Disciple* (1980), Isherwood recorded his surprise at meeting Heard again in Hollywood, for the London dandy had been transformed into an emaciated saint with a 'disconcertingly Christlike' beard, who 'wore jackets with ragged cuffs and jeans which had holes or patches at the knees'.[24] In a letter, Maria Huxley disparaged Heard's ostentatious asceticism: as she drove him home (Heard was too unworldly to learn to drive), she asked if he needed any supplies and Heard replied that he was fine, he had some stale bread and rotten fruit at home.[25]

Heard's holier-than-thou behaviour led to a temporary *froideur* in his friendship with Huxley. 'Aldous says [Heard] has taken up the attitude of "the Buddhist Party"', Maria writes to her sister,

> meaning that he's become as rigid as if he'd joined the Communist Party . . . Gerald has become the priest of this 'party-religion' and so one may no longer laugh even about his person . . . He can't see us because he will not leave his house for more than two hours at a time because of his meditations . . . Meditation takes for him the place of drugs.[26]

Another problem for Huxley was that Heard had begun to present himself as a guru, giving spiritual lectures at the Vedanta Center as well as Baptist and Quaker venues. While Huxley acknowledged that there were elements of Heard in the character of Propter, he noted that the latter was 'a more massive figure':[27] for where Propter's spiritual authority derived from his mystical experiences, Heard's vaunted asceticism and meditations had not resulted in a mystical breakthrough and thus he had to rely on his mundane knowledge of religious texts. Consequently, Huxley felt that Heard's adoption of the guru role was presumptuous, and he was dismayed by the sanctimonious attitude that led Heard to break off his association with the Vedanta Society on the grounds that Prabhavananda (who ate meat, smoked cigarettes and drove a car) was insufficiently ascetic in his lifestyle.[28] Isherwood maintained that Heard's problems with the Vedanta Center were more personal than theological: 'He recoiled from the women, with their chatter and laughter and bustle, because they were lively and vital and he was a life-hater.' Heard expressed disgust for the human body and affronted Isherwood by likening the penis to 'a bit of loose gut hanging down from the abdomen'.[29]

Despite their differences, it was Heard who suggested the subject of Huxley's next book, *Grey Eminence* (1941), a biography of François Leclerc du Tremblay (1577–1638), more commonly known as Father Joseph. The book reinforces the message of *After Many a Summer* that politicians, mired in the human world of personality and time, cannot apprehend good, much less effect it. Father Joseph began his career as a Capuchin monk who had had mystical experiences, but largely as a result of his immersion in politics and his collaboration with Cardinal Richelieu, his 'unitive life' came to an end and he began to feel forsaken by God. 'It was a dark night of the soul,' writes Huxley,

Christopher Isherwood (standing in the middle, wearing a tie), Swami Prabhavananda (seated in front of Isherwood) and Gerald Heard (seated to Prabhavananda's left) before the Vedanta temple at Ivar Avenue, *c.* 1940s.

but not that salutary dark described by St John of the
Cross, not the dark night of those who are undergoing the
final and excruciating purgation from self-will; no, it was
that much more terrible, because fruitless and degrading,
dark night, which is the experience of those who have seen
God and then, by their own fault, lost him again.[30]

The case of Father Joseph also illustrated Huxley's conviction that
devotional mysticism was misguided at best and dangerous at
worst. Huxley argued that Father Joseph's mystical experiences
'were not of the highest order' because of the Catholic approach to
mental prayer he had been taught by the English mystic Benet Fitch
of Canfield, who held that the proper subject of meditation was not
the impersonal godhead but Jesus and, in particular, the passion
of Christ.[31] 'Contemplation of persons and their qualities', writes
Huxley, 'entails a great deal of analytic thinking and an incessant
use of the imagination. But analytic thinking and imagination
are precisely the things which prevent the soul from attaining
enlightenment.'[32] Since Father Joseph was debarred from achieving
full mystical union, Huxley affirmed, he was unable to perceive the
evil results of his political machinations, which were designed to
destabilize the Habsburg Empire so that France might lead a united
Europe in a glorious crusade against the Turks. The long-range
repercussions of Father Joseph's actions were catastrophic: the
origins of the two world wars could be traced back, Huxley argued,
to the Thirty Years War, which paved the way for the French
Revolution, the Napoleonic Wars, German nationalism and the
balkanization of the Habsburg Empire.[33]

The only hope for humankind, Huxley asserted, was for mystics
to work in small groups on the margins of society, where they could
practice 'goodness politics', as opposed to working at the centre and
being corrupted by 'power politics'.[34] A good example of this was
St Benedict, who lived for three years in the mountains by himself

and emerged as a mystic who went on to found the Benedictine Order, which over the course of the Dark Ages 'civilized north-western Europe . . . provided the only educational facilities then available, and preserved and disseminated the treasures of ancient literature'.[35] However, Huxley's message that '[s]ociety can never be greatly improved, until such time as most of its members choose to become theocentric saints', did not sit well with secular critics.[36] For instance, Richard Chase in *Partisan Review* ridiculed Huxley's assertion that Father Joseph's 'antisocial conduct' was due to his devotional approach to mental prayer.[37] Even Julian Huxley and Bertrand Russell were 'alarmed' by the book, and asked Isherwood at a Hollywood party: 'Did he . . . do you mean to say he actually, er, really – *prays?*'[38]

While Huxley didn't pray, he had certainly continued his meditation practice after he'd vanquished his insomnia. It seems safe to assume, given the new-found emphasis in his work on the salvific benefit of mystical union, that he was hoping to achieve this through meditation, but it's hard to determine how long he meditated for, and how often. In 1935, when he'd just started meditating, he wrote to the poet Robert Nichols: 'The bore of this Yoga mind control is that it's so frightfully difficult and takes so long – also that it probably demands a pretty careful regulation of diet and sexual habits' (*LAH*, 389). In the yoga philosophy expounded by the Indian sage Patanjali, yogis are expected to observe five *yamas* or ethical restraints, including non-violence (*ahimsa*) and chastity (*brahmacharya*). While living in Hollywood, the Huxleys moved in a glamorous social circle, including Greta Garbo, Paulette Goddard, Charlie Chaplin, Salka Viertel and Anita Loos. According to Dunaway, Maria was part of the Hollywood lesbian scene known as the Sewing Circles, which included Garbo and her lover Mercedes de Acosta.[39] Maria also continued to make trysts for her husband with Hollywood 'starlets', so it seems that Huxley was far from celibate at this time.[40] Indeed, it was only later, after Maria was diagnosed with breast cancer in the early 1950s, that Huxley briefly became celibate. In a letter from that time, Maria writes: 'I no longer drive him to the string of beautiful women he used to sleep with.'[41] On the one hand, then, Huxley was convinced that goodness and peace could only be actualized by mystics, and thus it was the duty of every right-thinking man and woman to try to achieve this through meditation and asceticism; on the other hand, Huxley had a robust libido and found it hard to resist the opportunities afforded to a famous writer in Hollywood who, in his forties, was still a handsome man with a full head of hair. This perhaps accounts for the cognitive dissonance of *After Many a Summer*, with its gleeful descriptions of the flesh and the dour sermonizing of Mr Propter.

Since April 1939 the Huxleys had been living in Pacific Palisades, a suburb of Los Angeles adjacent to Santa Monica. But in December 1941 Maria began to have problems with her lungs and was told by her doctor to live in a dry climate, so Huxley bought a 16-hectare (40 ac) ranch in the Mojave Desert on the site of what had once been a socialist colony during the Great War, named Llano del Rio. Huxley paid for various improvements on the dilapidated house, and Maria moved into the new property in February 1942 while Huxley remained in Hollywood (staying with Eva Herrmann) to work on a screenplay of *Jane Eyre* for Twentieth Century-Fox. The Huxleys led a pretty frugal life at Llano: the electricity was provided by a noisy and unreliable generator. Following the American entry into the war after Pearl Harbor, there were food and fuel shortages; Maria wrote to her mother that they ate 'healthily but vaguely'.[42] There were fig, apple and pear trees in the garden, as well as tomatoes and grapevines. At this time, the Huxleys were both vegetarian, though this was for medical rather than spiritual reasons: Huxley had been plagued by bronchitis, as well as suffering outbreaks of hives and oedema, and had been put on a 'stringent meatless, sugarless and saltless diet' by his 'rather

Studio portrait of Huxley in the early 1940s.

crazy Viennese doctor' (*SL*, 381). Maria especially fell in love with Llano, and when they eventually moved on after the war she would forever regard it as a paradise lost. While living at Llano, Huxley noted after her death, Maria had had several mystical experiences: 'This was the reason for her passionate love of the desert. For her, it was not merely a geographical region; it was also a state of mind, a metaphysical reality, an unequivocal manifestation of God' (*LAH*, 735).

In November 1941 Huxley had begun work on a new novel, *Time Must Have a Stop* (1944), but ran into problems with it and decided instead to write a book about the Bates method. He no longer received an annual stipend from Chatto, for during the war writers who were not resident in Britain were prohibited from receiving advances of more than £50,[43] which made him reliant on his film work and his dwindling royalties. *The Art of Seeing*, though, proved to be an unexpected hit, selling all 10,000 copies of the initial print run in Britain within days of its publication and about 23,000 copies in America by September 1943.[44] Huxley's teacher, Mrs Corbett, was busy training men in the Bates method who had been rejected from the armed services on the grounds of their defective vision, with the result, Huxley writes to his brother, 'that scores of them get through their tests after only a few weeks, sometimes even a few days, of training' (*LAH*, 482–3). In the early 1940s Huxley had also tried and failed to write a genuine utopia set in the near future, which would feature a self-sufficient group of sages living on the margin of society,[45] in other words a fictional embodiment of the kind of spiritual community he had been promoting as the only hope for humankind.

Meanwhile, Heard was attempting to realize this kind of spiritual community in reality. In 1941 he purchased 121 hectares (300 ac) of land in the hills behind Laguna Beach in Orange County, California, and commissioned Isherwood's cousin Felix Green to build him a monastery, which was completed in 1942.[46] Trabuco

College was conceived by Heard as a non-denominational 'club for mystics', in which there would be no 'masters and disciples'.[47] In the Trabuco prospectus, which Jake Zeitlin affirmed was co-authored by Heard and Huxley, it is asserted that:

> The founders do not regard themselves as possessed of any
> special message or esoteric 'revelation.' Trabuco begins
> its work in a spirit of humble and open-minded enquiry.
> There are no 'prophets' among us. We all start from the
> beginning, bringing nothing but our need for God and our
> trust in His Grace, without which search for Him is vain.[48]

The residents at Trabuco were subject to a fixed routine: meditation from 6 to 7 a.m.; after breakfast (which was eaten in silence) the remainder of the morning was at the residents' disposal until another 'sit' (a spell of meditation) from 11.30 to 12.30; after lunch, residents were expected to carry out maintenance and gardening work; at 4 p.m. tea was served, which was followed by the final sit from 5 to 6; dinner was then served at 6.30.[49]

Huxley visited Trabuco six times between 1942 and 1943.[50] After his first visit, Maria wrote that he was 'delighted' with the place and reported that the rift between Huxley and Heard had been healed.[51] While women were allowed at Trabuco, Heard insisted on celibacy for the residents and married couples were only permitted to sleep together in a separate building. In a letter to Grace Hubble (wife of the astronomer Edwin Hubble), Maria likened the atmosphere at Trabuco not to a cloister, but to 'an English country house party', and opined that it would furnish the material for a good novel in the manner of *Crome Yellow*.[52] But Heard was not well suited to the guru role. Like Huxley, he was chary of too much human contact and unable to assert his authority. Furthermore, Trabuco did not generate the 'spiritual outcomes [Heard] had hoped for', which he regarded as a 'failure'.[53] Merely leading a monastic life and

Huxley and his friend the astronomer Edwin Hubble, *c.* 1940s.

meditating a lot does not guarantee that one will have a mystical experience; it is contingent, as Yama puts in the Katha Upanishad quoted above, on the 'grace of the Creator'. In *After Many a Summer*, Mr Propter invokes Matthew 22:14 ('many are called, but few are chosen') and affirms that the spiritual aspirant who wishes to achieve mystical union must practice not only 'unsleeping good-will but also unsleeping intelligence' and 'recollection' (an awareness or mindfulness of God's presence in the soul) (*AMAS*, 96–7). In 1947, with only a few residents left to maintain the estate, Heard closed Trabuco and a few years later gave the monastery and land to the Vedanta Society of Southern California.[54]

After completing *The Art of Seeing*, Huxley resumed work on *Time Must Have a Stop*, which he later considered his finest novel.

The message of the book is by now familiar: 'the final end and purpose of human existence' is to achieve 'unitive knowledge' with the timeless 'Godhead or Ground', which is the 'unmanifested principle of all manifestation' (*TMHS*, 282). The quotations are from Sebastian Barnack's 'minimum working hypothesis' concerning 'spiritual experience', but their function is more akin to a mystical manifesto. In the novel's epilogue, set in 1944, Barnack affirms that a 'shared theology is one of the indispensable conditions of peace', and that for 'obvious and odious historical reasons' it cannot be orthodox Christianity, Hinduism or Buddhism (*TMHS*, 287). In the absence of a common mystical religion, Barnack argues, humankind has fallen prey to pseudo-religions, such as fascism, communism and nationalism. Most Westerners now repose their faith not in God but in a utopian future, which they believe will come to pass as a result of technological progress, or with the extermination of the Jews or the bourgeoisie. But time makes a mockery of man's worldly ambitions. This is the thrust of the second clause in the quotation from Shakespeare's *Henry IV, Part 1*, which gives the novel its title:

> But thought's the slave of life, and life's time's fool,
> And time, that takes survey of all the world,
> Must have a stop.

The godhead or what Huxley was now calling the 'divine Ground' (this phrase derives from the German mystic Meister Eckhart) is eternal; unitive knowledge of the Ground requires a transcendence both of one's self and of time. It 'is only by deliberately paying our attention and our primary allegiance to eternity', writes Barnack in his notebook, 'that we can prevent time from turning our lives into a pointless or diabolic foolery' (*TMHS*, 286).

The novel begins, however, in 1928, when the seventeen-year-old Sebastian worships poetry and women. His father John Barnack is a puritanical political activist who is made to represent the futility of believing that society can be improved through political action. In contrast, his uncle Eustace embodies the unregenerate sensual man, who abandoned his political career to 'marry a rich widow with a weak heart', whose death allows him to indulge his taste for art, fine wine, prostitutes, cigars and Italian cuisine. As luck (or Huxley's artless plotting) would have it, the Barnacks just happen to be distantly related to a mystic, the second-hand bookseller Bruno Rontini, whose goodness derives from his unitive knowledge of eternity or the divine Ground. Huxley's revulsion from the body and sex is even more pronounced than in *After Many a Summer*, where it was undermined by his faintly tumescent descriptions of Virginia Munciple and the gambolling nudes of the Beverley Pantheon and Jo Stoyte's art collection. Sebastian loses his virginity to a prostitute, whose breath 'stank of beer and caries and onions' and for whom he felt, after the 'frenzied' act was over, a 'disgust' and 'horror as though for a corpse – and the corpse laughed and offered him its derisive condolences' (*TMHS*, 28). Afterwards the prostitute, regarding Sebastian's house, decides to double her rate, forcing him to borrow money from the elderly housemaid on pain of exposure.

Sebastian follows the same narrative trajectory as Anthony Beavis in *Eyeless in Gaza*, from sensual indulgence to a form of mysticism via guilt and the intervention of a guru figure. While visiting Eustace in Florence, Sebastian meets Veronica Thwale, who is acting as a companion to Eustace's mother-in-law Mrs Gamble. Veronica, reacting against the strictures of her Christian upbringing, defines the 'essence of life' as 'pure shamelessness', the 'physiological denial of reverence and good manners and Christianity' (*TMHS*, 146). When Veronica seduces him, sex is represented in terms of its 'essential shamelessness':

In his fancy, love had been a kind of gay, ethereal
intoxication; but last night's reality was more like
madness. Yes, sheer madness; a maniac struggling
in the darkness with another maniac.

'Twin cannibals in bedlam . . .' The phrase came to
him as he was examining the red and livid mark of teeth
on his arm. Twin cannibals, devouring their own identity
and one another's; ravening up reason and decency;
obliterating the most rudimentary conventions of
civilization. And yet it was precisely there, in that frenzy of
the cannibals, that the attraction had lain. (*TMHS*, 218)

Of all the women Sebastian subsequently sleeps with, the 'essential
shameless' with Veronica cannot be surpassed, and their intimacy
persists even after they both marry other people. When his wife
Rachel discovers that he is being unfaithful, she miscarries and
dies of blood poisoning. In spite of his guilty conscience, Sebastian
continues to sleep with Veronica, even though this means deceiving
his friend Paul De Vries (her husband), because she offers him 'an
experience of otherness almost as absolute . . . as the otherness
of God' (*TMHS*, 272). It is in this state of guilt-ridden self-loathing
that Sebastian once again encounters the mystic Bruno Rontini,
who, back in 1928, had been imprisoned by the Italian fascists on
account of Sebastian boasting to a corrupt art dealer of his father's
connection to the antifascist Professor Cacciaguida. It is Bruno's
radiant serenity and paradoxical vitality in the face of the throat
cancer that is killing him that inspires Sebastian to forsake his
former life of sensuality and embrace the mystical path, which
results in his formulation of the 'minimum working hypothesis'.

Huxley's disgust for the body can also be found in his
descriptions of Eustace's gluttony, in his 'large damp lips' that
slobber on the 'teat' of his cigars, that snuffle up lavish dinners,
that imbibe champagne, cognac and chianti. It is no accident

that Eustace dies of a heart attack while sitting on the toilet. The only thing 'more shameless than living', says Veronica, is 'dying' and its concomitant putrefaction (*TMHS*, 147). Huxley is justly celebrated for his depiction of Eustace's journey through the three *bardos* or intermediate states between death and rebirth. These are described in the *Bardo Thödol* or *Tibetan Book of the Dead*, a Mahayana Buddhist text which had first been published in an English translation in 1927 and was still relatively unknown in the West. The first *bardo*, the *chikhai bardo*, occurs at the moment of death, which is signified by the emergence of the 'clear light', a 'profound state of consciousness' caused by the dissolution of the ego in which mental concepts and duality fall away; if the deceased recognizes the clear light as reality, she achieves liberation from *samsara* (the cycle of rebirth).[55] But of course Eustace has no knowledge of Tibetan Buddhism and is unaware that he is dead, thus he experiences the clear light as a force from without that, while overwhelmingly blissful, threatens to obliterate his residual 'consciousness principle':[56]

> The whole of existence was brightness – everything except this one small clot of untransparent absence, except these dispersed atoms of a nothingness that, by direct awareness, knew itself as opaque and separate, and at the same time, by an excruciating participation in the light, knew itself as the most hideous and shameful of privations. (*TMHS*, 137)

Unwilling to relinquish these last vestiges of his selfhood, Eustace misses his chance to achieve nirvana and enters the *chönyid bardo* (the *bardo* of the experiencing of reality), where the deceased is subject to karmic apparitions. Given that the peaceful and wrathful deities the deceased traditionally encounters in the *chönyid bardo* are manifestations of her consciousness, Huxley substitutes for them Eustace's memories of the sacred and the sexual: for instance, a recitation of Mozart's *Ave verum corpus*, a motet based on the Latin Eucharistic hymn of the same name in praise of the true body of Christ. Huxley deliberately juxtaposes the divinity of Christ's true body with the sinful fleshly body of Eustace. After he and his lover Laurina listen to the *Ave verum corpus* in a church in Nice they drive to a casino in Monte Carlo, where they enjoy a lucky streak and cover the floor of their hotel room with the winnings. Eustace, sprawling on the money with Laurina, exclaims '*Ave Verum Corpus*', and laughingly reflects: 'This was the true body' (*TMHS*, 155). It is while Eustace is in the *chönyid bardo* that he is summoned to a seance being conducted by the medium Mrs Byfleet at the behest of his mother-in-law. Thanks to Mrs Byfleet, Eustace is able to re-experience embodiment, but his irreverent witticisms are misconstrued by Byfleet and Bettina (her spirit guide or 'control') as Christian platitudes. In a subsequent seance, Eustace enters the *sidpa bardo* (the *bardo* of rebirth), and, despite being privy to visions of the same old lust, death and suffering in the future, including one of his mother-to-be Mrs Weyl (one of the participants of the seance) being trampled to death before his eyes in a refugee retreat during the Second World War, he chooses rebirth over what he perceives to be the annihilation of the clear light.[57]

Eustace's refusal to surrender his consciousness principle is emblematic of the rest of humanity: until such time as we are prepared to make a determined effort to transcend our personalities and make contact with the divine Ground, we will be trapped in an endless cycle of war, conflict, desire and death – and social reforms, political revolutions and new technology will never ameliorate this all-too-human condition. Sebastian's 'minimum working hypothesis' is akin to Huxley's conception of the Perennial Philosophy, which formed the subject of his next book. *The Perennial Philosophy* (1945) is an anthology of mystical texts from most of the religious traditions over two millennia, from the *Bhagavad Gita* (*c.* 500 BCE–500 CE) and the Upanishads (*c.* 800–400 BCE), to the *Bardo Thödol* (*c.* eighth century CE), *The Cloud of Unknowing* (*c.* fourteenth century CE) and the Book of Common Prayer, including Christian saints, Taoist sages, Sufi mystics, Hindu philosophers and Buddhist poets. Much like Sebastian, Huxley affirmed that only a 'shared theology' afforded the basis for a lasting peace, and that the mysticism of the Perennial Philosophy provided this. It can be boiled down to four fundamental tenets:

> First: the phenomenal world of matter and of individualized Consciousness – the world of things and animals and men and even gods – is the manifestation of a Divine Ground within which all partial realities have their being, and apart from which they would be nonexistent.
>
> Second: human beings are capable not merely of knowing about the Divine Ground by inference; they can also realize its existence by a direct intuition, superior to discursive reasoning. This immediate knowledge unites the knower with that which is known.
>
> Third: man possesses a double nature, a phenomenal ego and an eternal Self, which is the inner man, the spirit, the spark of divinity within the soul. It is possible for a man, if he so desires, to identify himself with the spirit and therefore with the Divine Ground, which is of the same or like nature with the spirit.
>
> Fourth: man's life on earth has only one end and purpose: to identify himself with his eternal Self and so to come to unitive knowledge of the Divine Ground.[58]

Huxley provides illustrations of these tenets from mystics of many denominations. Space permits only a few examples of each.[59] Huxley argued that the teachings of mystics were exemplary because they derived from mystical union with the divine Ground, rather than religious dogma. For example, Meister Eckhart, in keeping with the first tenet, heretically held that there was an impersonal godhead or 'Ground of Being', which was the transcendent source of the Christian Trinity of Father, Son and Holy Ghost, from which the phenomenal world emerged or emanated. 'God and Godhead are as distinct as heaven and earth,' writes Eckhart. 'Heaven stands a thousand miles above the earth, and even so the Godhead is above God' (*PP*, 30). Likewise, in Advaita Vedanta, the godhead is *brahman*, which is the source of the Hindu trinity of Brahma, Vishnu and Śiva, whose roles respectively are creator, sustainer and destroyer of the cosmos.

In the second tenet, the 'direct intuition' that unites the knower with the divine Ground is mystical in nature, and it is from this mystical union that the mystics derive their teachings, which often contradict religious dogma (as was the case with Eckhart above). Huxley differentiates between two types of mystical experience: the 'way to Reality in and through the soul', which corresponds to Stace's introvertive experience, and the 'way to Reality in and through the world', which is akin to extrovertive experience (*PP*, 56). Somewhat surprisingly, Huxley gives almost no examples of mystical experience and focuses instead on the similarity of the mystics' teachings, so my examples of each 'way' are taken from another source. St Teresa exemplifies the way to Reality through the soul: 'In the orison of union', she writes,

> the soul is fully awake as regards God, but wholly asleep as regards things of this world and in respect of herself. During the short time the union lasts, she is as it were deprived of every feeling . . . she is utterly dead to the things of the world and lives solely in God.[60]

The way to Reality through the world is exemplified by this layperson's experience:

In that time the consciousness of God's nearness came to me sometimes . . . I felt myself one with the grass, the trees, birds, insects, everything in Nature. I exulted in the mere fact of existence, of being a part of it all – the drizzling rain, the shadows of the clouds, the tree-trunks, and so on.[61]

The ultimate way is to obtain enlightenment through the soul and then to go forth into the world (rather than shut oneself up in a monastery) and use one's insight into the true nature of things to help others achieve the same goal.

The best example of the third tenet is the affirmation that *atman* and *brahman* are one, which can be found in the Upanishads and was examined above. The Perennial Philosophy fitted seamlessly with monistic traditions such as Advaita Vedanta, but Huxley had to work much harder to find plausible examples from the Abrahamic religions and Buddhism. For example, in Islam, it is heretical to claim an identity between God and humans, and Huxley had to content himself with the following anecdote to illustrate the third tenet: when someone knocked on his door and asked if the Sufi saint Bayazid of Bistun was there, he replied: 'Is anybody here except God?' (*PP*, 12). For 'Hinayana' Buddhists there is no self or soul, much less a godhead in the manner of *brahman*. Huxley attempted to resolve this by asserting that the clear light of Tibetan Buddhism (discussed above) was a 'Universal Mind'.

The fourth tenet proclaims that the ultimate goal of life is mystical: to achieve 'unitive knowledge of the divine Ground'. This knowledge will not only confirm the truth of the Perennial Philosophy, it is the key to salvation. Again, this fourth tenet jibes well with Advaita Vedanta but is less compatible with the Abrahamic religions, in which salvation is not contingent on mystical experience. For the orthodox Christian, who relies on dogma, prayer and ritual rather than mystical union for salvation, the best that can be hoped for is 'survival' in a posthumous 'heaven', but this offers no opportunity for 'immortality', which Huxley defines as 'participation in the eternal now of the divine Ground' (*PP*, 211). Both introvertive and some forms of extrovertive experience would afford this kind of 'immortality', but for Huxley the ideal is enlightenment, which usually denotes a permanent state of mystical identity in which the mystic perceives the godhead not only in the rarefied heights of her soul but in the multiplicity of the phenomenal world, and this mystical identity persists after the death of the body.

Huxley was also at pains to point out the 'ethical corollaries' of the Perennial Philosophy that had a direct bearing on the Second World War. For example, the goal for perennialists is the transcendence of time and the experience of eternity (the divine Ground). Huxley believed that the war and the besetting evils of his era were primarily caused by the 'idolatrous worship of things in time', such as technology, the nation and the self (*PP*, 95). Human beings embraced their time-bound egos and were largely ignorant of their eternal *atman*. Indeed, the ego was the chief obstacle to unitive knowledge of the Ground, since this required charity and self-abnegation. Rather than worshipping God, or the impersonal godhead of the Perennial Philosophy, people idolatrously worshipped their nation, and uncritically accepted their nation's divine right to colonize other countries and wage war against them for the greater glory of the nation, and this had led to the outbreak of two world wars in Huxley's lifetime. Belief in God had largely been usurped by a belief in progress, and thus salvation was no longer sought in the eternity of the divine Ground but in the future, and the realization of this revolutionary or utopian end justified the employment of the most rebarbative means in the present. Technological progress had produced the 'four-motor bomber loaded with white phosphorus and high explosives' (*PP*, 79) and had been achieved by the instrumental exploitation of nature; the Perennial Philosophy, in contrast, emphasized the immanence as well as the transcendence of the godhead, and inspired an attitude of reverence and respect for animals and nature. What was paramount for perennialists was not the promise of a Brave New World in the future, it was the experience of eternity in the present.

6

Following the Tao, 1945–54

Huxley completed *The Perennial Philosophy* in March 1945 and it was published in September, selling 23,000 copies in a matter of weeks, which was surprising, given the subject matter.[1] In June Huxley purchased a chalet in the small town of Wrightwood, located in the valley of the San Gabriel Mountains, at an altitude of 1,800 metres (6,000 ft). For the past two years Huxley had been suffering from an allergic reaction to poison ragweed, which he had contracted at Llano; consequently, he had been forced to spend more and more time in Los Angeles, at a rented apartment on South Doheny Drive. As with Llano, though, the Wrightwood cabin required considerable renovation; thus Huxley purchased the neighbouring house, which was in better condition. That first summer at Wrightwood, he invited Krishnamurti and his long-term lover Rosalind Rajagopal to stay in the cabin. In her memoir of Krishnamurti, Rosalind's daughter Radha fondly recalled their time at Wrightwood: the long walks in the woods, tea at the Huxleys' house, dinner prepared by her mother. Radha's father, Krishnamurti's friend and editor Desikachar Rajagopal, remained at Ojai, but joined them for the occasional weekend. The following year Krishnamurti purchased the Huxleys' chalet and used it as a summer retreat.[2]

With the end of the war, there was an uptick in Huxley's film work. He was commissioned by Walt Disney to write a treatment for a partially animated film of *Alice's Adventures in Wonderland*, which would also include episodes from Lewis Carroll's life. Huxley's mother Julia Arnold had been photographed by the Rev. Charles Dodgson (Carroll) as a girl and the idea of faithfully re-creating the intellectual milieu of Oxford in the 1860s was appealing.[3] But it seems Huxley's cerebral approach did not suit Disney, who ended up dropping the biographical episodes and concentrating on the cartoon version of Alice's adventures. Huxley was also trying to get a film version of *Brave New World* off the ground, with his friend Paulette Goddard as producer and her husband Burgess Meredith in one of the roles. The trouble was that RKO, having purchased the film rights for a mere $750 when the novel was published, now wanted $50,000 for them, which made the project untenable.[4] While there have been several lacklustre made-for-TV movies of *Brave New World*, it has yet to receive the full cinematic treatment; at one time, the director Ridley Scott was attached to the project with Leonardo DiCaprio slated to star as the 'Savage', but the film was never made. A more successful enterprise was Zoltan Korda's film of Huxley's short story 'The Gioconda Smile' (1921), for which Huxley wrote the screenplay. Korda directed and produced the film, which was to Huxley's liking, though he was dismayed that the studio retitled the film *A Woman's Vengeance*.

Huxley had been contemplating writing a historical novel set in the fourteenth century; it is perhaps regrettable that he abandoned it in favour of *Ape and Essence* (1948), which is one of his most vilified works. Part of the problem is the book's ungainly structure, which starts like a conventional novel, with a nameless narrator working unhappily in Hollywood, who discovers a rejected scenario titled 'Ape and Essence' by William Tallis, with the scenario composing the remainder of the book. Huxley later confided to a correspondent who had questioned the form of *Ape and Essence* that he had tried to 'write it "straight"' in a realist manner, but had been unsatisfied with the result and had adopted the scenario form to make it more 'fantastic' (*LAH*, 600). In the past, Huxley had proved adept at writing the grotesque – for example, the comic

Photograph by Lewis Carroll of Huxley's mother, Julia, standing next to her sister Ethel.

episodes from Henry Wimbush's history in *Crome Yellow* or the play performed in the cabaret in *Antic Hay* – but the grotesque aspects of the scenario fall flat in *Ape and Essence*.

At the outset of the book, the nameless narrator is ruminating on the assassination of Mahatma Gandhi, who is presented as a saint who refused to hold himself aloof from politics and became embroiled in the 'subhuman mass-madness of nationalism', and was killed as a result (*AE*, 6). This is a variation on the theme of *Grey Eminence*. The title of Tallis's scenario derives from Shakespeare's play *Measure for Measure*:

> But man, proud man,
> Drest in a little brief authority,
> Most ignorant of what he is most assur'd,
> His glassy essence, like an angry ape
> Plays such fantastic tricks before high heaven
> As make the angels weep.

This dualism between the body, with its animal instincts, and the soul seems at first very much in keeping with *Time Must Have a Stop*. As a result of his apelike appetites, Tallis ends up shunning humanity and living alone in the Mojave Desert, where he dies (like the gluttonous Eustace Barnack) in the bathroom from a heart attack. When the narrator attempts to track down Tallis he is met by Mrs Coulton, who had rented Tallis her house. According to Coulton, Tallis married a German woman before the Great War, whom he divorced, leaving her and their daughter in Germany, while he returned to America and married an actress, who subsequently left him. His ex-wife and daughter died (Coulton says she thinks they were Jews, who presumably perished in the Holocaust), and Tallis wrote the scenario to raise some money to send to his granddaughter. From these facts, the narrator invents the following history for Tallis: his first wife was frigid, and he abandoned her for a sensuous American actress, who turned out to be a 'bitch'. For 'the sake of physical pleasure', Tallis 'had condemned a wife and a daughter to death at the hands of maniacs, and a granddaughter to the caress of any soldier or black marketeer with a pocketful of sweetmeats' (*AE*, 22).

Tallis's scenario is set in Los Angeles in the year 2108, a hundred years after a third world war involving nuclear and biochemical

weapons. One of the more irksome aspects of *Ape and Essence* is
the arch narrator of the scenario, who occasionally breaks into
verse in the manner of a Greek chorus, and who describes a number
of scenes in which scientists, such as Albert Einstein, are enslaved
by apes and made to serve their lust for power. 'Surely it's obvious',
announces the narrator:

Doesn't every schoolboy know it?
Ends are ape-chosen; only the means are man's.
Papio's procurer, bursar to baboons,
Reason comes running, eager to ratify;
Comes, a catch-fart with Philosophy, truckling to tyrants;
. . .
Comes, rhyming and with Rhetoric, to write his orations;
Comes with the Calculus to aim his rockets
Accurately at the orphanage across the ocean;
Comes, having aimed, with incense to impetrate
Our Lady devoutly for a direct hit.[5] (*AE*, 32–3)

For more than two decades Huxley had been writing about the
ways in which science, philosophy, religion and rhetoric could be
made to serve pernicious 'ape-chosen' ends, but it seems that after
the Second World War and the advent of the atomic bomb he was
running out of patience and felt the need to underline his message.

As with *After Many a Summer* (1939), sex and religion are closely
intertwined. In the aftermath of World War III, the population of
Los Angeles have forsaken God and worship the devil Belial. One
of the many ironies of the religion of Belial is that it is even more
sexually repressive and misogynistic than Christianity. Women are
regarded as 'vessels of the Unholy Spirit', and are routinely whipped
for their 'Malicious Animal Magnetism', in other words the lustful
thoughts they inspire (*AE*, 71).[6] Although Belial is responsible for the
sexual impulse, women are nonetheless blamed for the deformed

babies that result from the genetic mutations caused by radiation: infants with more than three pairs of nipples and seven digits on a hand or foot are sacrificially killed in the 'Purification' ceremony and their mothers whipped with a 'pizzle' (a bull's penis). Sexual intercourse is forbidden except for a period of two weeks a year, which leads to carnal abandon in the population, and Huxley gleefully depicts the orgies that erupt on Belial Day. In order to avoid all temptation, the demonic clergy are castrated and attend to practical matters during the mating season while the laity are in rut.

The main focus of the scenario is a sexually repressed scientist named Alfred Poole, who has been emotionally crippled by an overbearing mother (much like Brian Foxe), who denies the body (at 38 he is still a virgin) and lives in his head (like most of Huxley's heroes). After becoming separated from the other members of the 'New Zealand Re-Discovery Expedition to North America', Poole is captured by Belial worshippers and narrowly escapes being buried alive by offering his botanical expertise to help improve their crops. Poole's aborted burial represents a rebirth for him: amid the sexual tumult of Belial Day, Poole embraces the body, falls in love with a nubile young woman named Loola and is given an insight into his 'glassy essence' by reading Shelley.[7] The fact that sex is part of this spiritual rebirth is highly significant and reverses the narrative trajectory of Huxley's recent heroes, such as Sebastian Barnack and Anthony Beavis, who abstain from sex in order to follow the mystical path.

At this time Huxley was increasingly influenced by Taoism, which celebrates nature and the world. The Tao (literally path or way) is akin to *brahman*, in that it is an impersonal godhead that has both immanent and transcendent aspects. The formless, unmanifest Tao gives rise to the One, an emanation that is manifest in time and space. The One gives birth to the Two, namely *yin* and *yang*, the dynamic interdependent poles of cosmic energy. The creative flux between these cosmic poles or principles gives birth to the 'Ten Thousand Things', in other words the phenomenal world.[8] But *yin* and *yang* are not a conventional Cartesian 'dualism, but rather an explicit duality expressing an implicit unity', namely the Tao.[9] Alan Watts defines the Tao as the 'flowing course of nature'. Taoists strive to embody *wu-wei*, the principle of 'non-action', which Watts defines as 'going with the grain, rolling with the punch, swimming with the current'.[10] In *The Perennial Philosophy*, Huxley writes that for Taoists

> personal sins and social maladjustments are all due to the fact
> that men have separated themselves from their divine source
> and live according to their own will and notions, not according
> to Tao – which is the Great Way, the Logos, the Nature of
> Things, as it manifests itself on every plane from the physical,
> up through the animal and the mental, to the spiritual. (*PP*, 115)

In *Ape and Essence* there are several references to the 'Order of Things', which is affirmed as the opposite of Belial. For instance, the Arch-Vicar maintains that history is the story of 'Man pitting himself against Nature, the Ego against the Order of Things, Belial . . . against the Other One' (*AE*, 90). In a letter written at the beginning of 1948, Huxley explicitly refers to 'Chinese Taoism, with its concept of an Order of Things' (*LAH*, 579). In *Ape and Essence*, then, the 'Order of Things' stands for the Tao, and Belial is the personification of man's God-eclipsing egotism. All Huxley's bugbears, the 'lunatic dreams of Progress and Nationalism' and the world wars to which they give rise, are attributed to the influence of Belial: 'Not I', intones the Arch-Vicar, 'but Belial in me' (*AE*, 97).[11]

After rescuing a volume of Shelley's work from a pile of books due to be burned in order to make bread, Poole develops a Taoist feeling for nature. 'There are times', says the narrator, after describing the distant mountains through Poole's eyes, 'when the world seems purposefully beautiful, when it is as though some mind in things had suddenly chosen to make manifest, for all who choose to see, the supernatural reality that underlies all appearances' (*AE*, 141). And Loola, and her body, are part of nature too; she is not a fallen woman, as his Christian mother would have judged her, much less a 'vessel of the Unholy Spirit'. Poole perceives Loola through a Romantic lens as 'a mortal shape indued / With love and life and light and deity' (*AE*, 123). As a result, he is emboldened to defy the Law of Belial and arranges clandestine trysts with Loola after the mating season is over. After quoting a passage from *Prometheus Unbound* in which the protagonist is described as a 'spirit of keen joy', the narrator reflects:

> Joy is only for those whose life accords with the given Order of the world. For you there, the clever ones who think you can improve upon that Order, for you, the angry ones, the rebellious, the disobedient, joy is fast becoming a stranger. Those who are doomed to reap the consequences of your fantastic tricks will never so much as suspect its existence. Love, Joy and Peace – these are the fruits of the spirit that is your essence and the essence of the world. But the fruits of the ape-mind, the fruits of the monkey's presumption and revolt, are hate and unceasing restlessness and a chronic misery tempered only by frenzies more horrible than itself. (*AE*, 142)

When Loola worries that Belial will discover their love (the punishment for sex outside the mating season is being buried alive), Poole reassures her that the 'Order of Things', in other words the Tao, will always prevail over Belial (the God-eclipsing egotism of humans), since 'whenever evil is carried to the limit, it always destroys itself'. In the long term, the 'Order of Things' always 'comes to the surface again'; in the short term, individuals 'can always work with the Order of Things' (*AE*, 148). In this spirit, Poole and Loola set off for Fresno to join the community of 'Hots' (individuals who feel the stirrings of libido all year round, rather than during the mating season).[12]

Huxley finished *Ape and Essence* in February 1948. Four months later, he and Maria were aboard a Cunard liner bound for Cherbourg. The first stop was Paris to see Maria's sister Jeanne and her husband Georges Neveux. The Huxleys were delighted to be back in Europe, and spent some weeks in Sanary; in a letter to Matthew, Maria mentions the possibility of moving back there the following year. In October the Huxleys were back in London, where they caught up with old friends, including Mary Hutchinson. Since Huxley's move to America, there had been a cooling of their friendship, with Huxley's last letter to Hutchinson in November 1942 offering his condolences on the death of her husband. In a letter from 1947, Maria wrote to Jeanne that she had no desire to renew her friendship with Hutchinson, and described Mary and her daughter Barbara as 'nymphomaniacs'.[13] But in the aftermath of the trip to Europe, Huxley writes to Hutchinson: 'It was wonderful to find such a warmth of affection after all these years' (*SL*, 400).

Shortly after his return, Huxley came down with bronchitis and spent the winter in Palm Desert, a city in the Coachella Valley, not far from Palm Springs. Llano had been sold and Wrightwood was inundated with snow during the winter. Moreover, Maria had suffered from altitude sickness at Wrightwood, but had put up with it for Huxley's sake. In May 1949 they purchased a house on North Kings Road, and after spending the summer at Wrightwood, moved there in October. For David Bradshaw, Huxley's return to Los Angeles, after the wilderness years in the desert at Llano and in the mountains of Wrightwood, was symbolic of Huxley's 'vacation of the ashram in favour of a revitalised concern with the social and political welfare of mankind'.[14] During the war years, Huxley had been chiefly preoccupied with 'mak[ing] the world safe for mystical experience' (*SL*, 361); now that the war was over, he seemed ready to concede that perhaps some good might be achieved in the strictly human world of time and craving by non-mystics. In this, he may have been inspired by his brother Julian, who in 1946 became the first director-general of UNESCO (the United Nations Educational, Scientific and Cultural Organization).[15] Huxley's letters to Julian during this period are full of ruminations and suggestions, such as this from December 1946:

> I wonder if there is any hope, through Unesco, of persuading the technologists, when they apply the results of pure science to industry, to remember that the sabbath was made for man and not vice versa; that human beings with certain physical and psychological needs come first and that applied science should serve those needs and those human beings and should not compel the human beings to be the slaves of applied science and its capitalistic or governmental owners and managers. (*LAH*, 557)

In his post-war work, Huxley exhibited a new and prescient concern with ecology. Hitherto, his interest in population levels had revolved around the differential birth rate, with the masses outbreeding the middle and upper classes, which eugenicists feared would lead to the degeneration of the population. In his essay 'The Double Crisis' (1948), he expressed his alarm that the population of the earth was rising by '200 million every 10 years', while food supply was dwindling as a result of widespread soil erosion, which was rapidly reducing the arable land of the U.S., Australia, Asia and South America to dust. Huxley predicted that by the year 2000 the population would be around 3 billion.[16] In fact, the population of the world in 1999 was 6 billion and is currently over 7 billion.[17] What Huxley failed to foresee was that soil erosion could be reversed with synthetic fertilizers, and more food could be produced per acre through new technologies, such as genetically modified crops. Nonetheless, Huxley's central message is even more pertinent today than it was in 1948, and, as with *Ape and Essence*, we can see how Huxley's interest in Taoism helped to shape his attitude to nature and the environment:

Treat Nature with charity and understanding, and Nature will repay you with unfailing gifts. Treat Nature aggressively, with greed and violence and incomprehension: wounded Nature will turn and destroy you . . . The Chinese taught that the Tao . . . was present on every level from the physical and the biological up to the spiritual; and they knew that outrages against Tao, in Nature no less than in man, would lead to fatal results. We have to recapture some of this old lost wisdom. If we fail to do this – if, presumptuously imagining that we can 'conquer' Nature, we continue to live on our planet like a swarm of destructive parasites – we condemn ourselves and our children to misery and deepening squalor and the despair that finds expression in the frenzies of collective violence.[18]

During the winter at Palm Desert, Huxley had written a stage version of *Ape and Essence*, which he then translated into French, but neither of these plays was performed. In 1950 he collaborated with Isherwood on a scenario titled 'Below the Equator',[19] set in South America, but, like their previous collaboration *Jacob's Hands*, this failed to attract a Hollywood studio. *Jacob's Hands* was written in 1944 and concerns a faith healer; it was apparently based on a ranch hand who healed animals at Llano. Jacob starts by helping animals but is persuaded to try his healing powers on humans, too. When he symbolically heals the heart of the millionaire Earl Medwin, Medwin steals Jacob's girlfriend Sharon; thoroughly disillusioned, Jacob reverts to healing animals. 'It's easy enough to cure the body,' says Jacob. 'But how many can cure the soul?'[20] This treatment was thought to be lost; however, in the 1990s the American actress Sharon Stone read about the collaboration in Isherwood's diaries and got in touch with Huxley's second wife Laura, who unearthed it in a box of souvenirs.[21]

In April 1950 Huxley's son Matthew, now thirty years old, married the documentary film-maker Ellen Hovde in New York. Initially Matthew had studied medicine (the career choice marked out for his father) at Colorado University. He was then drafted into the medical corps of the U.S. Army in March 1942, but was invalided out a few months later due to German measles; while recuperating at Llano, he confessed to his parents that he'd never wanted to be a doctor and had only taken pre-medicine at Colorado to please them, whereupon it was agreed that he should choose his own career.[22] During this period of cohabitation, tensions arose; Huxley vented his frustration in a letter to Matthew from Hollywood, in which he attempted to adopt a paternal tone. 'If you go to Ojai,' he writes, to spend some time with Krishnamurti, 'I feel very strongly that you should make the event an occasion for reorganizing your existence altogether.' He petulantly notes that Matthew is selfish and intolerant, but what sticks in Huxley's craw is Matthew's habit of allowing 'the purposeless reading of an intrinsically worthless magazine article, to get in the way of doing a present duty or thinking rationally about the future'. He instructs his son to be a less 'promiscuous' reader, and to concern himself with the best that has been thought and said (*LAH*, 497–8). There followed a brief stint of work at Warner Brothers as a reader, after which Matthew majored in Latin American studies at the University of California at Berkeley. At the time of his marriage he was working for the Conservation Foundation of New York (now known as the Wildlife Conservation Society).

After Matthew's marriage, the Huxleys made another trip to Europe. From Julian's house in Hampstead, Huxley writes to Isherwood in July that 'England is much more cheerful than it was 2 years ago' (*LAH*, 627), presumably due to the gradual process of derationing that had begun in 1948. Julian organized a family reunion of 27 relatives, which Huxley enjoyed, despite the elegiac 'Proustian atmosphere' of lost time (*LAH*, 629). He spent part of August at Sanary, but, perhaps due to an enervating heatwave, the glamour of their previous trip was gone, and, rather than moving back there permanently, as Maria had mooted, they sold the house the following month.[23]

Back in America, the Huxleys investigated alternative therapies and parapsychology. In December 1950 they tried dianetics, a self-help psychology created by the science-fiction writer L. Ron Hubbard, and which would later be incorporated into Scientology. Hubbard maintained that there was a conscious 'analytical mind' and an unconscious 'reactive mind'. Traumatic events from childhood, the prenatal state and even past lives were stored in the reactive mind in the form of 'engrams', and could produce all kinds of mental and psychosomatic distress. The purpose of dianetics was to purge these engrams from the reactive mind through the 'auditing' process, producing a state of optimal mental health known as 'clear'.[24] Huxley reports that while 'Maria has had some success in contacting and working off engrams and has been back repeatedly into what the subconscious says is the pre-natal state', he himself was 'completely resistant' to the auditing process. Huxley describes Hubbard as 'curiously repellent physically' and 'a very queer fellow – very clever, rather immature and in some ways rather pathetic' (*SL*, 416–17). Huxley and Maria also tried 'E-Therapy', developed by the psychotherapist and Buddhist scholar A. L. Kitselman in the 1950s. The aim of the therapy is to bypass the conscious ego and access the unconscious in order to solve mental or psychosomatic problems. The subject is put into a 'light hypnotic trance' and guided by an observer, who facilitates the release of repressed memories, physical tension and intuitive answers to urgent problems (*LAH*, 648, 650). Maria writes to her sister that

Aldous is transfigured and this, I think, is due to E-Therapy. I have a rapport with my E, I know it is all true . . . but Aldous was blocked and it took him a long time to reach his E, his deeper inner self. This therapy is a simple and rapid way to the recommendations of the saints.[25]

At around this time, Huxley and Maria held regular Tuesday-night gatherings at their house on North Kings Road, at which the guests observed or participated in hypnotism, seances and the paranormal. One of the mediums they observed was Eileen Garrett, whom Huxley had met in the years of the Great War when she ran a tea room in Hampstead.[26] She was investigated by the American Society for Psychical Research in 1931 and was one of J. B. Rhine's first research subjects; in fact, she went on to fund Rhine's parapsychology laboratory at Duke University with money provided by one of her clients, Congresswoman Frances P. Bolton, one of the richest women in America at the time.[27] In 1951 Garrett established the Parapsychology Foundation in New York and hosted an annual parapsychology conference in Saint-Paul de Vence, which Huxley attended in 1954 and 1961.[28] The psychiatrist Humphry Osmond (who introduced Huxley to mescaline) was present at one of their Tuesday nights and witnessed the medium Sophia Williams, who emitted 'strange little voices', and who served as inspiration for the Huxley story 'Voices' (1955).[29] On a subsequent visit, Osmond witnessed the hypnotic regression of one of Huxley's guests to previous incarnations.[30] Huxley also practised hypnotism on himself and others. In a letter from 1952, he writes that 'three or four years ago' an intestinal infection had left Maria in a state of 'nervous exhaustion', and that she found relief in hypnotherapy. Since then, he had become a 'good hypnotic operator' and had been using it to help Maria recover from various ailments (*LAH*, 646–7). In addition, Huxley was interested in UFOS. Writing in response to Gerald Heard's book *The Riddle of the Flying*

Saucers: Is Another World Watching? (1950), he informed Matthew that two physicists who came to visit him from Caltech 'regarded the disc saucers as real' and argued that UFOs were not detectable by radar since they used 'electro-gravitational waves' (*SL*, 424). As for himself, he was keeping an open mind.

Huxley began writing his next non-fiction book, *The Devils of Loudun* (1952), in November 1950. In 1629 Jeanne des Anges, the prioress of the convent of Ursuline nuns in the French town of Loudun, became obsessed with the parish priest Urbain Grandier. Being cloistered, Sister Jeanne had never seen Grandier, but his reputation as a womanizer had led her to imagine him as a 'mythical figure, part Jupiter, part Satyr – bestially lustful and yet, or therefore, divinely attractive', and by and by her unavowable fantasies led to a psychosomatic stomach disorder (*DL*, 121). After Grandier refused Sister Jeanne's offer to become the convent's spiritual director, he began to show up in her dreams, importuning her with unspeakable suggestions; by way of warning, Sister Jeanne repeated these febrile dreams to her fellow nuns and soon two of the sisters were receiving nightly apparitions from the goatish Grandier. Following Grandier's rejection, Sister Jeanne had invited one of his enemies to become the new spiritual director: Canon Mignon hated Grandier because Grandier had seduced Mignon's niece. Mignon arranged for three exorcists to visit the nunnery, and before long it was common knowledge in Loudun that the nuns were all possessed by devils as a result of Grandier's pact with Satan. There followed several months of exorcisms, many of which were performed in public by yet another exorcist, the Satan fanatic M. Barré, who administered a 'miraculous enema' in front of the prurient citizens of Loudun in order to purge Asmodeus, one of the seven devils that were plaguing Sister Jeanne (*DL*, 130). Eventually, Grandier was accused of sorcery but the magistrate ruled that it was all a matter of suggestion, superstition and, on Mignon's part, malice, which was only exacerbated by the endless round of

Portrait of Huxley by the American novelist Donald Windham.

exorcisms. Changing tack, Grandier's enemies identified him as the author of a scurrilous attack on Cardinal Richelieu, who promptly ordered a new investigation of the devils of Loudun, following which Grandier was charged, and this time convicted, of sorcery. Although he was gruesomely tortured for this crime (the bones in his feet and legs were systematically broken) in order to extract a confession, Grandier heroically maintained his innocence to the very end and was burned alive.

In *Devils* Huxley emphasized the contemporary relevance of Grandier's demonization and pointed out that while the idea of evil manifesting in a sorcerer now struck us as quaint, in the more secular twentieth century evil had been represented as residing in communists in America, Jews in Germany and capitalists in the Soviet Union. The following year, Arthur Miller's play *The Crucible* (1953) was produced on Broadway, which similarly portrayed the Salem witch trials of 1692 as a metaphor for the persecution of communists by the House Un-American Activities Committee. Huxley counterpointed the story of the libertine Grandier with that of the zealous Jesuit Jean-Joseph Surin, who was sent to Loudun in December 1634, four months after the immolation of Grandier, to exorcize Sister Jeanne. Huxley portrayed Surin as a contemplative who had vainly pursued mystical union through physical austerities, which had resulted in neurosis and a number of psychosomatic disorders, such as headaches and 'intense muscular pains' (*DL*, 265). This, and the fact that he was completely convinced by the diabolic possession of the nuns, left him vulnerable to contagious hysteria, and presently he, too, was possessed by a devil. Surin's possession, though, was far from continuous; in the lucid intermissions he continued to exorcize Sister Jeanne, until his health broke down in October 1636, and he was forced to return to Bordeaux. While the last of Sister Jeanne's devils departed the following year, Surin's 'possession' would last for 25 years. He was afflicted with a partial paralysis of the body, which rendered him unable to undress, so that for twenty years he slept in his clothes and, in order to avoid vermin, changed his shirt once a week – an agonizing process that took him several hours. Eating was also a torture for him, and if he managed not to throw up the little he was able to ingest, he was plagued by dyspepsia.

At this time, Huxley was drawn to world-affirming traditions, such as Taoism, in which nature is regarded as a divine emanation, and this may well have influenced his portrait of Surin. According to Huxley, the root of the problem was Surin's Christian conception of the world and nature as fallen, created *ex nihilo* rather than efflorescing out of the divine substance of God. And human beings, saddled with original sin, were part of this fallen nature. Father Lallemont, Surin's instructor at the Jesuit college he attended in Rouen, fervently believed in the 'total depravity of fallen nature' and routed the 'natural man' within by a course of self-mortification so extreme it led to his premature death (*DL*, 89–90). Huxley took a dim view of asceticism and argued that 'it is only through the *datum* of nature that we can hope to receive the *donum* of Grace' (*DL*, 330); by attempting to transcend the body, to turn away from nature, Surin was in fact keeping God at arm's length. Significantly, Surin's only mystical experiences, as a young man at Jesuit college, were of God as immanent in the world: 'I went out into the garden of our college at Bordeaux; and so great was this light that I seemed to myself to be walking in paradise' (*DL*, 353). As the physical symptoms of Surin's 'possession' finally began to abate in the late 1650s, he became sensible again of the natural world. He abandoned his austerities and was once more able to apprehend the divine Ground in the world. On the evidence of 'certain passages' in his last book of 'devotional writings', Huxley maintained that at the end of his life Surin achieved enlightenment: 'for one more soul, the Kingdom [of God] had come on earth' (*DL*, 353).

Work on *Devils* was interrupted by ill health. In March 1951 Huxley came down with flu, which led to iritis, temporarily depriving him of sight in his bad right eye. Unable to tolerate sunlight, Huxley had to sit in a darkened room. In addition to the often debilitating pain of the disease and the intermittent headaches, Huxley was terrified that the infection would spread to his good eye, leaving him totally blind, and sought treatment from his friend Leslie LeCron, a psychotherapist who specialized in hypnotism, in order to manage his anxiety.[31] Huxley began to recover in the autumn and resumed work on his book. In October, Matthew and Ellen had a baby boy, whom they named, at Huxley's suggestion, Mark Trevenen. At the beginning of 1952 Maria underwent an operation to remove a mammary cyst, which turned out to be malignant. The cancer had spread to her pre-lymph nodes: Maria was told that the prognosis was poor, but refused to tell Huxley that she was probably going to die, perhaps not wanting to believe it herself. At any rate, friends and family were informed that the operation was a success and that she would make a full recovery.[32]

Huxley finished *Devils* in January 1952 and it was published in October. In the appendix, he dilated on the necessity of self-transcendence. Given the arduous nature of 'upward self-transcendence' to mystical union, Huxley noted that historically humans have exploited all the means available for 'downward self-transcendence' through music, crowds, sex and especially drugs. 'From poppy to curare', he writes,

> from Andean coca to Indian hemp and Siberian agaric, every plant or bush or fungus capable, when ingested, of stupefying or exciting or evoking visions, has long since been discovered and systematically employed . . . To go beyond the limits of the insulated ego is such a liberation that, even when self-transcendence is through nausea into frenzy, through cramps into hallucinations and coma, the drug-induced experience has been regarded by primitives and even by the highly civilized as intrinsically divine. (*DL*, 362)

This discussion of the link between drugs and spiritual experience set the table for his next book, *The Doors of Perception* (1954). Huxley had first written about mescaline in the essay 'A Treatise on Drugs' in 1931. It was inspired by his reading of *Phantastica* by the German pharmacologist Louis Lewin, who had first encountered peyote (from which mescaline is derived) in 1886. Lewin noted that peyote was venerated as a god by the Mexicans and Native Americans who used it as a sacrament. His description of the visionary effects of mescaline doubtless reminded Huxley of accounts of extrovertive mystical experience: 'Quite ordinary objects appear as marvels. In comparison with the material world which now manifests itself, the ordinary world of everyday life seems pale and dead. Colour-symphonies are perceived. The colours gleam with a delicacy and variety which no human being could possibly produce.'[33]

Huxley's interest in mescaline revived in 1953 as a result of the work of the British psychiatrists Humphry Osmond and John Smythies. Huxley had read some of their articles and had been corresponding with Smythies since November 1952.[34] At this time, Smythies and Osmond were investigating the psychotomimetic (psychosis-mimicking) properties of the drug, and had both taken it in order to gain a deeper insight into the experience of schizophrenics. When Osmond first took mescaline, he was oppressed by feelings of persecution and paranoia: the people he met in the streets of London had deformed faces 'covered with wens', the 'wide spaces of the streets were dangerous' and the 'houses threatening'.[35] Osmond's 'set', a term used by psychedelic researchers to denote the subject's beliefs and expectations, was that mescaline would mimic the symptoms of schizophrenia and so his experience largely reflected this.

But Huxley had quite different ideas about the effects of mescaline and was clearly hoping for some sort of spiritual experience. In his first letter to Osmond on 10 April 1953, a month *before* he took mescaline, Huxley predicts that in the future mescaline may play a role in the education of young people, enabling them to 'taste and see' the visionary worlds found in the works of poets, mystics and painters (*LAH*, 669). At the end of the letter, Huxley invited Osmond (who was working at the Saskatchewan Hospital in Canada) to stay at his house when Osmond attended a psychiatric conference in Los Angeles. At Huxley's request, Osmond brought some mescaline with him and supervised Huxley's first trip on 4 May 1953. After ingesting 400 mg of the drug, Huxley notes the transfiguration of the three flowers in a vase in his study: 'I was not looking now at an unusual flower arrangement. I was seeing what Adam had seen on the morning of his creation – the miracle, moment by moment, of naked existence' (*DP*, 15). The rose, iris and carnation in his study did not signify the concept of, or the signified, 'rose', 'iris', 'carnation' – they signified 'is-ness', a 'transience that was yet eternal life, a perpetual perishing that was at the same time pure Being, a bundle of minute, unique particulars in which, by some unspeakable and yet self-evident paradox, was to be seen the divine source of all existence' (*DP*, 15–16). Shifting his attention to the furniture of his study, Huxley experienced a 'sacramental vision of reality':

> I was back where I had been when I was looking at the
> flowers – back in a world where everything shone with the
> Inner Light, and was infinite in its significance. The legs,
> for example of that chair – how miraculous their tubularity,
> how supernatural their polished smoothness! I spent several
> minutes – or was it several centuries? – not merely gazing at
> those bamboo legs, but actually *being* them – or rather being
> myself in them; or, to be still more accurate (for 'I' was not
> involved in the case, nor in a certain sense were 'they') being
> my Not-self in the Not-self which was the chair. (*DP*, 19)

What Huxley is here describing is one of the key features of mystical experience: the transcendence of the self and the concomitant identification with the divine Ground. Huxley identifies himself with the chair legs, yet in doing so he has transcended his self and realizes that the chair legs, far from signifying mere 'chair legs', are in fact a manifestation of the divine Ground. This is what he is trying to articulate in his slightly cumbersome phrase: 'being my Not-self in the Not-self which was the chair'.

In reflecting on his mescaline experience, Huxley borrowed ideas from key thinkers associated with psychical research, namely

C. D. Broad, Henri Bergson and William James, all past presidents of the SPR, who argued that the brain acts as a filter rather than a producer of consciousness. In *The Doors of Perception*, Huxley refers to the divine Ground as 'Mind at Large': he asserts that human beings are in constant contact with Mind at Large and that the brain filters this omniscient stream of consciousness through a 'reducing valve' in order to prevent it from being 'overwhelmed and confused' by this cosmic data dump, leaving only 'a measly trickle of the kind of consciousness which will help us to stay alive on the surface of this particular planet' (*DP*, 19–20). Huxley speculates that mescaline inhibits the enzymes that supply the brain with glucose, thereby impairing the efficiency of the reducing valve, which filters Mind at Large, and which consequently admits a greater portion of cosmic consciousness. If Huxley's theory was correct, however, hypoglycaemics would be especially susceptible to mystical states, which is not the case. More recent studies have shown that there is a 'similarity between the chemical structures of psychedelics and neurotransmitters', which would 'affect the transmission of signals between brain cells', producing a comparable effect to the widening of Huxley's reducing valve.[36]

The filter thesis or model of mind initially seems counter-intuitive. Surely it's the human *brain* that produces consciousness, rather than 'Mind at Large'. But for all the advances in cognitive science, neuroscience and the much-vaunted promise of AI, scientists are still unable to explain how the physical brain gives rise to a metaphysical consciousness. A good analogy is to compare the brain to a computer, which subjectively filters the Internet, and leaves behind traces of its activity in the form of cookies (which record Internet searches and preferences). Someone with no knowledge of the Internet would assume that the information the computer user accessed came from inside the computer rather than wirelessly via the abstract concept known as the Internet. Likewise, for those of us with no first-hand knowledge of mystical union, it is easy to assume that consciousness originates in the brain rather than the abstract concept of the divine Ground or Mind at Large. For Huxley, the mystic in a state of mystical union enjoys a kind of broadband access to Mind at Large. It is from this ineffable experience that mystics derive their wisdom, insight and authority. In Huxley's model, psychics and mediums are granted greater access to Mind at Large, much less than mystics but much more than ordinary consciousness, and this enables them to read other people's minds, or to describe memories attached to objects and places, or to view the future or the past (since in Mind at Large there is no time and past, present and future are melded into eternity).[37]

Taking mescaline was for Huxley a spiritual breakthrough. Although he had been meditating since the mid-1930s, he hadn't come close to the mystical experiences he wrote about with such facility that some reviewers assumed he'd had them himself. Hitherto, he had known 'contemplation only in its humbler, its more ordinary forms', such as 'rapt absorption in poetry or painting', but on mescaline he experienced 'contemplation at its height' (*DP*, 33–4). It was one thing to know, in theory and at second hand, that the godhead was immanent in the world, and quite something else to experience it for himself. It reinforced Huxley's post-war predilection for traditions, such as Taoism and Zen Buddhism, which placed a premium on divine immanence. In a letter from 1949, Huxley writes that 'Zen interests me more and more', particularly its emphasis on 'nature as a manifestation of the divine'; it also shuns the devotionalism to which the Vedanta Society 'seem[s] to be succumbing' (*SL*, 409). Even though Advaita Vedanta held that there was an immanent, as well as a transcendent, aspect of *brahman*, the devotionalism of the Vedanta Society swamis, who conceived of the godhead in terms of a personal deity whom they worshipped in a shrine, had the effect of privileging the transcendent aspect of *brahman*. As a result of this emphasis on transcendence and on liberation from the world through meditation, Huxley came to regard Advaita Vedanta as life-denying.[38] Huxley's mescaline experience marked the start of the Tantric turn in his work, in which he presented the body and the world as divine, and which reached its apotheosis in *Island* (1962).

7

Death and the *Moksha*-medicine, 1954–63

Around autumn 1953 Maria had a second operation on her breast and began a new round of radiation treatments.[1] There is no question from Huxley's letters that he was aware of the situation, for he writes to Osmond in December about Maria's 'malignancy' and its possible 'metastases' (*LAH*, 690). In spite of Maria's condition, they travelled to France in April 1954. In Paris, Maria consulted with an eminent specialist who was a friend of her brother-in-law Georges Neveux. Maria told this doctor not to tell Huxley of her prognosis, since he had begun a new novel – *The Genius and the Goddess* (1955) – and required equanimity to write. On the one hand, Maria confided to Jeanne and Georges that she was resigned to dying, but on the other she felt she must stay alive as Huxley would not be able to cope without her.

Huxley gave a paper on the 'Other World' of visionary experience evoked by mescaline at Eileen Garrett's parapsychology conference in Saint-Paul de Vence. This paper would become the kernel of *Heaven and Hell* (1956), a companion essay to *The Doors of Perception*. 'The typical mescalin[2] or lysergic acid experience', Huxley writes,

> begins with perceptions of coloured, moving, living geometrical forms. In time, pure geometry becomes concrete, and the

visionary perceives, not patterns, but patterned things, such as carpets, carvings, mosaics. These give place to vast and complicated buildings, in the midst of landscapes, which change continuously, passing from richness to more intensely coloured richness, from grandeur to deepening grandeur . . . Almost never does the visionary see anything that reminds him of his own past. He is not remembering scenes, persons or objects, and he is not inventing them; he is looking on at a new creation. (*HH*, 78–9)

These visions are usually experienced with the eyes closed. *The Doors of Perception* is chiefly concerned with the transfiguration of the outside world Huxley experienced with his eyes open, and he often downplayed the visionary aspect of his mescaline experiments – however, in a letter to Osmond, he writes of the 'moving geometries' of his first mescaline session as being 'highly organized and, at moments, very beautiful and significant' (*LAH*, 779). These visions, Huxley posited, derived from the collective unconscious, and were characterized by intense colours, lights and internal significance. In this respect, visionary experience resembled descriptions of the heavens and fairylands of folklore and myth, such as the Garden of the Hesperides, Eden, Avalon, Elysium, the Islands of the Blest. The reason, Huxley speculated, that we prize gemstones in this world, such as diamonds and rubies, is that they remind us of the unearthly luminosity of the Other World we unconsciously glimpse at our mind's antipodes. For some people, on the other hand, psychedelic substances transport them not to a visionary heaven but to a visionary hell, revealing an 'Indwelling Horror', rather than a divine immanence (*HH*, 107). This is the pathological landscape of the schizophrenic. But where the mescaline taker, when overwhelmed with the terrifying intensity of the experience, can reassure himself that the effects of the drug are only temporary, the schizophrenic is trapped in a 'reality which he is not holy enough to live with', and eventually he has recourse to the 'most desperate counter-measures, from murderous violence at one end of the scale to catatonia, or psychological suicide, at the other' (*DP*, 46).

After a brief tour of the Middle East, taking in Ismailia, Cairo, Jerusalem, Beirut and Cyprus, the Huxleys visited Sybille Bedford in Rome, who reported a transformation in Huxley's bearing and appearance. 'I had never seen Aldous look less vulnerable'; he possessed a new-found 'authority'; his presence had a 'peace-inducing effect'; he was 'in some new way extraordinary'.[3] Bedford attributed this change to his paranormal investigations, and to the hypnotism he practised on Maria and himself, but I would argue that it was more likely the result of his mescaline experience. In *The Doors of Perception*, Huxley notes that 'the man who comes back through the Door in the Wall[4] will never be quite the same as the man who went out'. He 'will be wiser but less cocksure, happier but less self-satisfied', at peace with the 'unfathomable Mystery' of the cosmos (*DP*, 64). Furthermore, in 1955, Gerald Heard confided to Isherwood that taking mescaline was 'the greatest experience he had ever had'.[5]

Laura Archera, the former violinist turned psychotherapist who would become Huxley's second wife, drove them to the Etruscan tombs in Tarquinia, which Lawrence had lyrically evoked in *Sketches of Etruscan Places* (1932). Huxley had first met Laura in 1948, when she impulsively decided that he must write the screenplay for a documentary film she was hoping to produce. While the film never got made, Laura spent a delightful afternoon with the Huxleys in Wrightwood and subsequently connected with them at social events in Los Angeles.[6] In her biography, Bedford recalled that during their stay in Rome, Maria had a long conversation with Laura, and later voiced her suspicion that in that tête-à-tête Maria designated Laura as her successor.[7] But while Laura recollected that night in her memoir, she merely stated that Maria told her she felt she would 'live a little longer', and was trying to eat more to build up her strength.[8]

In July 1954 they spent three weeks with the Neveux at a rented house in Dieulefit, in the southeast of France. For Jeanne and Georges, knowing that Maria did not have long to live, the holiday was devastating, and it was only made worse by having to dissemble the situation to Huxley, who seemed delighted with the house and settled down to work in the garden on *The Genius and the Goddess*. There were surely enough clues for a perceptive man like Huxley to glean if he wanted to, but the idea of Maria's death must have been so unthinkable that he repressed it in order to remain in a state of wilful ignorance. The day after Huxley's sixtieth birthday, Maria's condition worsened; she arranged another consultation with the doctor in Paris, who told her to return to New York post haste. But they were unable to book another passage before 21 August, and rather than remain with Maria in Paris, Huxley rather callously left her behind to spend three weeks with Julian and Juliette in London. Thankfully, Jeanne's daughter Sophie was living in Paris and kept Maria company in the evenings. During the war, Sophie had been sent to live with Aldous and Maria in Los Angeles. According to Sophie, Maria never once complained or showed any signs of distress beyond downing a glass of whisky in her hotel room when ordinarily she never drank.[9] It seems odd, given how little time she had left, that Maria did not accompany Huxley to London, for she was very fond of Juliette, whom she had befriended during the war years at Garsington, where they had both met their future husbands.

Humphry Osmond made his second visit to the Huxleys in North Kings Road in November. In a letter to his wife, Osmond provides a fascinating insight into the importance of Maria's humanizing role in Huxley's life:

> Aldous is very shy and also very self-centered. He is also enormously intelligent. He peeks at people like a bacteriologist examining queer bugs . . . He could very easily

become, what brother Julian seems to be, almost ahuman. That he has not done so is, I think, due to Maria whose unselfishness and humanity has acted as a lens of Aldous' weak spiritual as well as his physical vision . . . Without her I think that his great intelligence might have drifted away from any real contact with the world of human beings.[10]

Huxley had planned to take mescaline again under Osmond's supervision, but was prevented from doing so by a case of shingles. In January 1955 Huxley was visited by one of Osmond's contacts, 'Captain' Al Hubbard, a Vancouver businessman and scientific director of the Uranium Corporation, who organized a mescaline session with Huxley, Heard and a friend of his called William Forthman. 'For five hours', Huxley writes, 'I was given a series of luminous illustrations of the Christian saying, "Judge not that ye be not judged", and the Buddhist saying, "To set up what you like against what you dislike, this is the disease of the mind"' (*LAH*, 720). For the last few years Osmond had been unsuccessfully applying to various foundations to fund a project he called 'Outsight', which would recruit a group of around a hundred prominent artists, writers and intellectuals to take a psychedelic substance and write up a report of the experience, much as Huxley had done for Osmond. Huxley hoped that with Hubbard's proselytizing enthusiasm and business connections, he would be well placed to secure funding for Outsight, but this never came to pass.

Meanwhile, Maria's cancer had spread to the spine, but Huxley was told it was lumbago and seemed perplexed that it required hospital treatment. In February, when Maria's 'jaundice' (that is, liver cancer) did not respond to treatment, he asked her doctors whether the 'malignancy is in the liver' but they prevaricated (*LAH*, 730). Finally, on 5 February, Huxley was told the truth: 'The news is very bad,' he writes to Matthew and Ellen. The 'malignancy has suddenly, almost explosively, started to spread – is in the liver and the lungs, and probably in the spleen and intestines too'. It seems that Maria was unaware that Huxley had been fully apprised of the situation, for he writes that Maria maintains that her symptoms are due to 'radiation sickness', and asks Matthew to pretend that he has been given an 'unexpected vacation' when he comes. 'I try not to cry when I see her, but it is difficult – after thirty-six years' (*SL*, 458–9). Maria returned home on 7 February, and was cared for by two nurses. In a letter that was circulated to friends after Maria's death, Huxley writes that their friend Leslie LeCron made some hypnotic suggestions to Maria, which banished the nausea that had made intravenous feeding necessary in hospital. Huxley also made hypnotic passes over her and repeated LeCron's suggestions, as well as urging her towards the clear light of the void. At 3 a.m. on 12 February, Huxley was summoned by the nurse to Maria's bedside. He repeated his suggestions, urged her to leave the body behind, to let go, to move forward into the light, and when she died three hours later it was 'with wonderful tranquillity' (*SL*, 459).

The Genius and the Goddess was published in June. The title has a Lawrentian ring, like *The Virgin and the Gypsy*, and Lawrence was much on Huxley's mind when writing the novel, as the inspiration for the eponymous goddess, Katy Maartens, was Frieda Lawrence. In particular, Katy shares Frieda's ability to restore her husband to health with her boundless pagan vitality. 'Thanks to Frieda', Huxley wrote to the actor who was to play Katy in the ill-starred stage adaptation, 'Lawrence remained alive for at least five years after he ought, by all the rules of medicine, to have been in the grave' (*LAH*, 831). It is no coincidence that Katy adores the early novels of Lawrence. The novel is largely narrated by John Rivers, who is recalling for a friend on Christmas Eve his involvement with the renowned physicist Henry Maartens some three decades previously. The Rivers of 1921 is an archetypal Huxley hero, a 28-year-old virgin with a manipulative widowed mother, whose attitude to sex is conditioned by his Lutheran upbringing. Rivers moves to St Louis to take up a research-assistant post with Henry and lodges in his house, where he promptly falls in love with Henry's wife. Under Katy's pagan influence, Rivers abjures his spiritualizing Christian background, and, like Lawrence, begins to worship life. 'I remember how he looked at landscapes', says Rivers, referring to his younger self,

> and the colours were incomparably brighter, the patterns
> that things made in space unbelievably beautiful. I
> remember how he glanced around him in the streets,
> and St Louis, believe it or not, was the most splendid city
> ever built. People, houses, trees, T-model Fords, dogs at
> lamp-posts – everything was more significant. (*GG*, 34)

This is reminiscent of Huxley's mescaline experience. It was also the visionary way in which Lawrence had apprehended the world. In his essay on Lawrence, Huxley writes: 'He looked at things with the eyes, so it seemed, of a man who had been at the brink of death and to whom, as he emerges from the darkness, the world reveals itself as unfathomably beautiful and mysterious.'[11]

Katy embodies what Rivers terms 'animal grace', which is rude good health, living in harmony with the Tao on a physical and biological level (*GG*, 75). Katy's animal grace is undermined when her mother becomes terminally ill. While Katy is nursing her in Chicago, Henry goes to pieces and comes down with a psychosomatic illness. Like many of Huxley's scientists, Henry is an emotional dunce, and he becomes convinced that Katy (who is twenty years younger than him) is having an affair with her mother's doctor. Due to Henry's precipitate decline, Katy is forced to return to St Louis, but when she arrives, exhausted by the stress of caring for her mother, whom she has had to abandon on the brink of death, she is a phantom of her former self. Her animal grace is gone and she is powerless to heal her husband. Katy has sex with Rivers in order to regain what Beulah (the Maartens's maid) calls her 'virtue', and to save Henry's life:

> She had to become part once more of the natural, and therefore divine, order of things. She had to re-establish her contacts with life – with life at its simplest, life in its most unequivocal manifestations, as physical companionship, as the experience of animal warmth, as strong sensation, as hunger and the satisfaction of hunger. It was a matter of self-preservation. (*GG*, 68–9)

The virgin Rivers is simultaneously ecstatic, shocked by the carnal appetite of the woman he had idolized as a goddess (more Artemis than Aphrodite, evidently), and wracked with guilt over their adultery. But while Rivers is stuck in the world of Christian dualism, Katy is 'beyond good and evil': from her 'goddess-eye viewpoint nothing had happened that was not entirely natural', and she feels no compunction about cheating on Henry (*GG*, 69). In the morning, her 'virtue' is restored (Beulah even says that she had prayed for 'Grace'), and as a result Henry begins to recover.

In retrospect, Rivers judges that both reactions – his own guilt and Katy's Olympian indifference – were wrong. Animal grace, Huxley asserts in *The Perennial Philosophy*, while it can be occasionally enjoyed by humans as a 'holiday from self-consciousness', is for animals. 'Man's nature is such that he must live a self-conscious life in time, not in a blissful sub-rational eternity on the hither side of good and evil' (*PP*, 167). The moral of the novel is that we must also be receptive to 'human grace' (such as the guidance of a guru) and 'spiritual grace', which derives from the godhead and makes mystical experience possible (*PP*, 167–8). Hence Katy's purely animal grace is portrayed as insufficient to a 'situation with which only a thorough-going Christian or Buddhist could adequately deal' (*GG*, 68). With her revitalized animal grace,

Katy is able to facilitate her husband's recuperation, but she kindles her daughter's jealousy (the teenage Ruth is in love with Rivers), and Katy crashes the car while arguing with her over, it is implied, Ruth's accusations of adultery, killing them both.[12]

In the aftermath of Maria's death, Huxley led what he termed an 'amputated' existence. He collaborated on a stage version of *The Genius and the Goddess* with the screenwriter Betty Wendel. From May to June, he was based in New York, where he caught up with friends, such as Osmond and Eileen Garrett. In a letter to the psychic Elise Murrell, Huxley writes that 'Maria has appeared to [Garrett] several times since her death', and passed on the following messages: 'I didn't hear the whole of the Bardle', that is the *Bardo Thödol*, and 'I found the Eggart . . . very helpful', meaning Meister Eckhart, whose phrase, 'The eye with which we see God is the same as the eye with which God sees us', Huxley had repeated to Maria while she was dying (*LAH*, 747).

Huxley spent the summer of 1955 in a rented holiday house in Connecticut with Matthew and Ellen, who had had a baby girl named Tessa in October 1953. 'How I admire people who can cope with children!' he writes to Bedford with bemusement (*LAH*, 762). There he worked on *Heaven and Hell*, which was published the following year. At the end of the book, while speculating on the afterlife, he writes:

My own guess is that modern spiritualism and ancient tradition are both correct. There *is* a posthumous state of the kind described in Sir Oliver Lodge's book, *Raymond*; but there is also a heaven of blissful visionary experience; there is also a hell of the same kind of appalling visionary experience as is suffered here by schizophrenics and some of those who take mescalin and there is also an experience, beyond time, of union with the divine Ground. (*HH*, 111)

Only a tiny minority, Huxley concedes, are capable of union with the divine Ground. A few will be able to withstand the 'visionary bliss of heaven'; a few will be subjected to the 'visionary horrors of hell'; but the vast majority will end up in Summerland (the spiritualist heaven), from where, he posits, they can eventually graduate to mystical union with the divine Ground (*HH*, 110–11). Huxley evidently envisaged Maria as being in transit from Summerland (where she could communicate with mediums) to the divine Ground, for he writes that Garrett had informed him that Maria had no intention of visiting dead relatives, which 'is typical of her, for she longed above all to be allowed to love the ultimate Love directly and uninterruptedly' (*LAH*, 747). During the 1950s Huxley had become fascinated by the paranormal, and these post-mortem messages from Maria may have spurred him on to join the SPR in 1956.[13]

In October Huxley took mescaline with Laura Archera. He had been in regular contact with her since Maria's death. Laura maintained that the reason Huxley was able to bear Maria's loss with such fortitude was because he was able to die to the past and live fully in the moment.[14] He had recently read of a man who had taken LSD with Al Hubbard, which had catalysed the recall of traumatic memories, and Huxley was keen to access parts of his childhood that were hidden to him. Indeed, he had already had a therapy session with Laura while Maria was alive in hopes of recalling a two-year period from the age of eleven that he felt he needed for his writing, but with no success.[15] In a letter to Osmond recounting the experience, he describes Laura as a 'dianetic operator', and says that 'Dianetic procedures' were attempted but failed to unravel any new memories. Nonetheless, Huxley's third mescaline experience far surpassed the others. What he had found troubling about his first experience was that it robbed him of his volition, and consequently, in his spellbound contemplation of the transfigured flowers in his study, he lost interest in his fellow human beings. This was the attitude of 'the *arhat*' or contemplative of 'Hinayana' Buddhism, who pursues nirvana by renouncing the world and concentrating on meditation (*DP*, 34). In *The Doors of Perception*, Huxley unfavourably contrasted the *arhat* to the *bodhisattva*, the exemplary figure in Mahayana Buddhism, who approaches nirvana by living in the world (as opposed to retiring to a monastery), and who elects to remain in *samsara* (the world of rebirth) in order to help others along the spiritual path. The breakthrough with Laura was that Huxley's former quietism was replaced by compassion:

what came through the closed door was the realization – not the knowledge, for this wasn't verbal or abstract – but the direct, total awareness, from the inside, so to say, of Love as the primary and fundamental cosmic fact. The Words, of course, have a kind of indecency and must necessarily ring false, seem like twaddle. But the fact remains . . . I was this fact; or perhaps it would be more accurate to say that this fact occupied the place where I had been. The result was that I did not, as in the first experiment [with Osmond], feel cut off from the human world. I was intensely aware of it, but from the standpoint of the living, primordial cosmic fact of Love. And the things which had entirely occupied my attention on that first occasion I now perceived to be temptations – temptations to escape from the central reality into false, or at least imperfect and partial Nirvanas of beauty and mere knowledge. (*LAH*, 769)

This, Huxley felt, was what the *bodhisattvas* had experienced, whereas in *The Doors of Perception* he had characterized his experiences as 'visionary' in nature.

In January 1956 Huxley and Heard had another mescaline session, this time under the supervision of the psychiatrist Howard Fabing. Huxley experienced a strong upwelling of grief and wept for the first time since Maria's death. According to Matthew's wife

Ellen, Huxley had repressed his memories of his mother, and the mescaline enabled him to remember her and grieve for her loss.[16] In the New Year, Huxley suggested to Laura that they should get married and they agreed on a date in March. The previous year, on a car journey with Maria's sister Rose, Huxley had been tickled by the drive-in wedding chapel in Yuma, Arizona, and the idea of a no-frills ceremony also appealed to Laura. While waiting for the minister, Laura worried that Huxley would expect 'the same total dedication' that Maria had shown him, and said: 'You know, darling, I love others, too.'[17] Prior to marrying Huxley, Laura had been in a long-term relationship with Virginia Pfeiffer, whose sister Pauline was Ernest Hemingway's second wife. When Huxley and Laura moved into a new house in Deronda Drive in the Hollywood Hills, it was partly to be near Virginia and her two adopted children. To Laura in the wedding chapel, Huxley diplomatically replied: 'It would be awful if you didn't.'[18] While eating lunch in a restaurant after the wedding, they were approached by a couple of journalists. This greatly perturbed Huxley, who had neglected to inform family or friends that he was getting married, including his son. Judging from *Eyeless in Gaza*, Huxley had been mortified by his father's second marriage (three years after Julia's death) to a woman thirty years his junior, but this did not prevent him from marrying Laura, whom he describes in his belated letter to Matthew as 'twenty years younger than I am' (Laura was 44; Huxley 61), just over a year after Maria's death. 'I had a sense for a time that I was being unfaithful to [Maria's] memory,' writes Huxley in the same letter. 'But tenderness, I discover, is the best memorial to tenderness' (*LAH*, 794). Matthew was understandably upset at having to read the news in the papers, and hated Laura, who got the lion's share of Huxley's royalties after his death.[19] Some of Huxley's friends were also unhappy about his marriage to Laura. 'I do not like her,' writes Isherwood in his diary. 'There is something shameful in Aldous's subjection to this mannish well-tailored bitch.'[20] On the other hand, Osmond visited Huxley and Laura in Los Angeles in November and found his friend in fine fettle: 'Aldous is, I think, happy, probably as happy as he has ever been,' he reported to his wife.[21]

After moving house in July, Huxley began mapping out his final novel, *Island* (1962). His plan was to portray a utopian society that combined humanistic science with a world-affirming spirituality. In a letter to Julian, he writes that most humans 'live at about twenty percent of capacity' and opines that a good religion should be a 'form of psychotherapy for the normal' that would enable individuals to realize a much larger swathe of their 'human potentialities' (*LAH*, 827, 829). But it was hard to make much headway with the novel due to several misguided theatrical projects (such as a musical version of *Brave New World*) that either amounted to nothing or ended in disaster. In addition, as a result of Huxley's growing eminence and age, he was importuned with requests to speak and lecture. He delivered two lecture series at the University of California, Santa Barbara, in 1959 on a wide range of subjects pertaining to the 'human situation', such as the 'destruction of natural resources, population growth', the juggernaut of new technology, the canker of nationalism, the nature of art and the 'actualization of latent potentialities' (*LAH*, 869). These lectures would be posthumously published in *The Human Situation* (1977). From March to April 1960 Huxley was visiting professor at the Menninger Foundation, a prestigious centre for psychiatry, at Topeka, Kansas. In a letter, Huxley describes the foundation as the 'Holy of Holies of Psycho-Analysis', and laments that in the clinic they treat their patients 'in the grand old Freudian way, as tho' they had no bodies – only mouths and anuses' (*LAH*, 888). In between times, he continued to work on *Island*, but worried that in order to convey the history and social structure of Pala (his fictional island) his slender narrative was saddled with too much exposition. In a letter to Matthew, he writes that he is 'haunted by the feeling that, if only I had enough talent, I could somehow poetize and dramatize all the intellectual material and create a work which would be simultaneously funny, tragic, lyrical and profound' (*LAH*, 875–6).

In May 1960 a lump on Huxley's tongue turned out to be malignant. The doctor recommended surgically removing one third of his tongue, which would have impaired his speech, and so Huxley consulted other specialists, and chose to have the cancer treated with radium needles inserted into the tongue. This treatment was successful, and had no effect on Huxley's voice, but it took him almost three months to recover.[22] He elected not to tell his family and friends, and after Maria's mother had accidentally learned he was in hospital he wrote to Matthew claiming that he had a nasty case of laryngitis. In the autumn semester, Huxley had another stint as a visiting professor, this time at the Massachusetts Institute of Technology (MIT). He delivered seven public lectures under the Shakespearian rubric 'What a Piece of Work Is Man'. The audience was mostly composed of students, from both MIT and other universities in the area, such as Harvard and Wellesley. When the lecture theatre was full, Huxley allowed two hundred more students to sit on the stage with him. Loudspeakers were set up outside the auditorium for the remainder of his lectures, enabling a further five hundred people to listen. Huxley also taught a seminar connected to the lectures to thirty undergraduates, and these were also packed to capacity by visitors and teaching staff.[23]

Huxley had recently been approached by the University of Texas, who wanted to buy his manuscripts and correspondence, and he had written to Matthew asking whether he wanted him to sell his papers now and donate the money to Trev and Tessa's education, or to hang on to them. Unfortunately, Matthew never got back to his father and when Huxley's house on Deronda Drive burned to the ground as a result of a bushfire in the canyon nearby all his papers were destroyed. Laura gives a curious account of it in her memoir. On the evening of 12 May 1961, she went to Virginia Pfeiffer's house to

Aldous with his second wife, Laura Archera, in the 1950s.

feed her cat. There she noticed the flames and smoke in the canyon below, but instead of rushing back to her house and informing Huxley, who was still writing, she stood there 'immobile, fascinated by the wild grace of the flames'.[24] After saving a box of Pfeiffer's papers, Laura went home and brought Huxley to Pfeiffer's house, wasting valuable time, and it only then occurred to Huxley that their own house might catch fire. A neighbour drove them to their house, and Huxley rushed in and rescued the manuscript of *Island* and a few suits. Laura meanwhile drifted through the house in a daze, and ended up saving her violin and a few clothes. She dreamily notes the 'cases of letters and diaries and notes for future writings' in the house, the voluminous correspondence between Huxley and Maria, but instead of attempting to rescue these, she and Huxley allowed themselves to be driven back to Pfeiffer's house by the neighbour.[25] Matthew was outraged by their behaviour. 'It's disgraceful,' he told Dunaway in an interview. 'She killed his background – his past life – and deliberately, as far as I'm concerned.'[26]

In the aftermath, Huxley moved into Gerald Heard's house in Santa Monica, where he finally finished *Island*. Many of his recent lectures had been concerned with what he termed 'human potentialities'. In one of them, Huxley had stated that 'the end of human life is to realize individual potentialities to their limits' and 'to create a society which makes possible such a realization'.[27] In these lectures, Huxley advocated investigating the viability of a number of potentially promising techniques that might improve education, well-being, creativity and cognitive efficiency. A few examples will have to suffice here.[28] Children should be given a 'differential education', Huxley argued, that recognized the psycho-physical classification of Sheldon (endomorph, mesomorph, ectomorph), and took into account Jung's distinction between the introvert and extravert attitudes. Education should also include the body, not just the mind – to this end Huxley recommended the Alexander technique and the Bates method. In these lectures, he also lauded gestalt therapy, and in particular the technique of getting patients to write sentences that began 'Here and now, I perceive', in order to cultivate awareness of the present. In *Island*, Palanese versions of these techniques and therapies are put into practice, and play an important role in the well-being of the population.

The keynote in *Island* is not on otherworldly salvation in 'heaven' but on self-actualization on earth, which is regarded as sacred or heavenly. As noted in the previous chapter, Huxley's world-affirming experiences on psychedelic drugs had led him away from Advaita Vedanta, which he perceived to be life-denying. In October 1956 he declined an invitation to speak at the Hollywood Vedanta Center on the grounds that he was not 'a joiner of churches' and felt uncomfortable assuming the guru role. For his part, Swami Prabhavananda regarded the idea that psychedelic drugs could induce mystical experience as a 'deadly heresy', and blamed Huxley and Heard for its dissemination.[29] While writing *Island*, Huxley had turned to the Tantric tradition for inspiration. In an interview from 1961, Huxley describes Tantra as the 'supreme doctrine' and deprecates Advaita Vedanta and 'Hinayana Buddhism' for their other-worldly emphasis on meditation, which excludes the world. In contrast, the point of Tantra and the 'later Mahayana doctrine is that it *includes* things, it permits you to live in the world – perceiving the absolute, perceiving nirvana . . . realizing it in acts of work and love'.[30]

In *Island*, the inhabitants of Pala engage in an experiential spirituality that celebrates the body and nature as sacred through the ritual use of the *moksha*-medicine (magic or psilocybin mushrooms) and the practice of *maithuna* (the yoga of love). For the first time in Huxley's fiction, sex is portrayed as a wholly positive experience. *Maithuna*, Ranga informs the visiting Englishman Will Farnaby, 'is the same as what the Oneida people called Male Continence' and 'what the Roman Catholics mean by *coitus reservatus*' (*1*, 77).[31] But '[i]t's not the special technique that turns love-making into yoga', he continues, 'it's the kind of awareness that the technique makes possible' (*1*, 78).[32] *Maithuna* is just one of the methods they employ to test the Sanskrit formula *tat tvam asi* 'you are That'. The phrase is found in the Upanishads, which constitute the key teachings of Advaita Vedanta; however, the idea of proving the validity of *tat tvam asi* through sexual intercourse would be heretical to the celibate swamis of the Vedanta Society. The Palanese strain of Mahayana Buddhism, Ranga explains, came not from Ceylon but from Bengal and Tibet and is therefore informed by Tantra. 'If you're a Tantrik', he tells Farnaby,

> you don't renounce the world or deny its value; you don't try to escape into a Nirvana apart from life, as the monks of the Southern Hinayana School do. No, you accept the world, and you make use of it; you make use of everything you do, of everything that happens to you, of all the things you see and hear and taste and touch, as so many means to your liberation from the prison of yourself. (*1*, 75–6)

In contrast to the Tantric, world-affirming Palanese, the villains of the book, the Rani and her son Murugan, advocate *brahmacharya* (sexual continence) in order to enhance their spirituality: 'Purity', says the Rani, 'is fundamental, Purity is the *sine qua non*' (*1*, 55). The Rani was educated in Switzerland, where she was introduced to Theosophy by the wife of one of her professors. She quickly proved to be an adept, and, in a manner reminiscent of the young Krishnamurti and Helena Blavatsky, began to take instruction from the Master Koot Hoomi. When Farnaby meets her, she is conspiring to sell Pala's oil concession in order to finance a 'World-Wide Crusade of the Spirit'. She has brought up her son to 'think of Woman as essentially Holy' and boasts of how, while she was lecturing abroad, the Palanese were unable to corrupt Murugan by sending first a girl his own age to seduce him, then, when she failed, an older woman. But Murugan's fortitude in this respect is a result of his homosexuality, rather than his adherence to *brahmacharya*.[33] While he deplores *maithuna* and pretends to be celibate, he is having an affair, Farnaby suspects, with Colonel Dipa. Reflecting on his meeting with Dipa, Farnaby recalls that the Colonel 'had been more than fatherly towards his young protégé, and towards the Colonel, Murugan had been a good deal more than filial – he had been positively adoring'. His suspicions appear to be confirmed when Dipa allows Murugan to drive his Mercedes: 'At the wheel of the Colonel's sports car Murugan was a maniac. Only an infatuated lover would have entrusted himself, not to mention his guest, to such a chauffeur' (*1*, 23).

The Palanese practice of *maithuna* is favourably compared to the asceticism of the Rani and the neurotic Western attitude to sex of Will Farnaby. Like many of Huxley's characters, Farnaby suffers from the Madonna–whore complex identified by Freud. After Farnaby's Aunt Mary, the 'only person [he] ever loved', dies of cancer, he perceives his fellow human beings as 'maggots' until he meets Molly, whom he describes as his aunt's 'successor' and marries out of gratitude for her kindness (*1*, 100). But Molly is a sexless 'Sister of Mercy' and Farnaby's attempts at lovemaking end in impotence, whereas he finds the 'mindlessness and vulgarity' of the plebeian Babs wildly exciting (*1*, 106). When he informs Molly that he is leaving her, she crashes her car and dies. But unlike Sebastian Barnack in *Time Must Have a Stop*, who renounces the world after the death of his wife in pursuit of an ascetic mystical path, Farnaby is enabled, under the *moksha*-medicine, to affirm the world as sacred. At first, he experiences a 'luminous bliss' with his eyes closed, which is simultaneously an 'understanding of everything', but with no distinction between knower and known, subject and object (*1*, 263). But Susila guides him away from this *arhat*'s nirvana of bliss apart from the world – 'Bodhisattvas dilute their Nirvana', she tells him, 'with equal parts of love and work' (*1*, 266) – and leads him to a point where, with his eyes open, he perceives nirvana in *samsara*: 'Will looked down at his burning bush and saw the Suchness of the world and his own being blazing away with the clear light that was also (how obviously now!) compassion' (*1*, 285).

Farnaby has been secretly working for the unscrupulous magnate Joe Aldehyde (who is anxious to appropriate Pala's oil), but he comes to treasure the Palanese people and refuses to betray them. Pala's utopian society has flourished by virtue of its geographical seclusion in the Indian Ocean, and hitherto its rajas have resisted the corrupting influence of capitalism. As a Theosophist, Murugan, the future raja, spurns the spiritual satisfactions of Pala (*maithuna* and the *moksha*-medicine) and is thus an avid convert to consumerism, and makes a deal with Colonel Dipa. The fact that Farnaby's epiphany comes as Murugan arrives with Dipa's soldiers for the *coup d'état* has led some critics to approach the novel from a Manichaean perspective and contend that Dipa and Murugan are the representatives of darkness triumphing over the good of Pala.[34] But in *Island*, Huxley emphatically rejects dualism in favour of the monism of Tantra and Mahayana Buddhism. In the Tantric scheme, Colonel Dipa and Murugan and the Rani are as much a manifestation of the godhead as the virtuous Palanese. For instance, Farnaby flippantly asks Susila if 'hunger and overbreeding and Colonel Dipa' are 'pure Suchness', and she replies: 'Of course' (*I*, 237). The mistake is to imagine that Pala is a paradise on earth, with Murugan as Eve inaugurating the Fall, whereas in Tantra the whole earth is Eden, and one of the functions of the *moksha*-medicine is to enable the Palanese to celebrate nature and embodied being as divine.[35]

The emphasis in *Island*, then, is unmistakably this-worldly: the goal, as Mr Menon puts it, is 'to live as fully human beings in harmony with the rest of life on this island at this latitude on this planet' (*I*, 210). According to Laura, *Island* was Huxley's 'ultimate legacy', in which he summarized the ways of living that would help people to achieve the full spectrum of their human potentialities, and he was 'appalled' that the critics treated it as a frivolous work of science fiction.[36] Huxley's message in *Island* is that we don't need to live in a utopian society like Pala to attempt to realize our human potential through the various techniques he elaborated, and that, with the additional help of psychedelic substances, we can strive to become fully human beings.

Huxley spent six weeks in England from June to July 1961, while Laura remained behind in Los Angeles, living in a rented apartment with Virginia Pfeiffer and her children. He took in some of the landmarks from his childhood, such as his mother's school, Prior's Field, and visited Hillside (his prep school) with his cousin Gervas. He had dinner with Sybille Bedford, who found him thinner and greyer but possessed of the animation and energy of a younger man. He wrote to Laura that London was somewhat sad since 'many of my old friends are either dead or ill or out of town'.[37] His love and tenderness for Laura are much in evidence in his letters to her, which begin 'My darling' and end 'Your A', and in which he refers to her as 'my sweetheart'. One senses a passion that had long been replaced by companionship with Maria, and it's a pity that only one of Huxley's letters to Maria has survived to compare the different modes of intimacy.

The following year, Huxley was visiting professor at Berkeley from February to May. It seems his schedule was less onerous than at MIT, for he found time for various conferences and lectures at Santa Barbara, Philadelphia, Colgate University, Los Alamos and Anaheim. Laura remained behind in the new house they now shared on Mulholland Highway with Virginia Pfeiffer and her children, tending to her psychotherapy practice. In July, Huxley had a swollen gland in his neck removed, which proved to be cancerous, and submitted to a course of radiation treatments. As soon as the latter were finished, he went to Brussels at the end of August for a meeting of the World Academy of Arts and Sciences. Although his doctor had been upbeat about his prognosis, Huxley made a dutiful tour of his and Maria's relatives in Belgium, Holland and England. He went to Godalming to visit Osmond, who had resigned his job as clinical director of the Saskatchewan Hospital and was about to take up a post at Princeton. Driving past Laleham, the house where he was born, with Juliette Huxley, they stopped and were shown around by the present owners. 'I felt that Aldous was very happy,' Juliette recalled.[38]

Huxley was back in Los Angeles at the end of September, where he hunkered down to finish his last book, the long essay *Literature and Science* (1963), which was his contribution to the two-cultures debate between C. P. Snow and F. R. Leavis about the relative importance of science and the humanities. Huxley argued that, on the one hand, men and women of letters should not turn their back on science like Keats for fear of unweaving the rainbow, and that, on the other, scientists should acknowledge that they dealt with but one aspect of the world (sense perception) while ignoring all the rest – the aesthetic, the spiritual, the emotional, the metaphysical and so on.

Huxley was diagnosed with cancer of the jawbone in April 1963. This was not a metastasis of his original tongue cancer, and indicated that, even with a radical operation, he would die sooner rather than later. He underwent another round of radiation treatments, which affected his vocal cords, enfeebling his voice. Nevertheless, Huxley flew to Stockholm for another meeting of the World Academy of Arts and Sciences at the end of July, followed by three weeks in London with Julian and Juliette. He looked so gaunt and spectral that Juliette arranged a consultation at Barts Hospital, but Huxley was dissembling his condition to all but Laura, Osmond and Virginia, and told Julian and Juliette that the doctor merely prescribed a rest.[39] In a letter to Matthew, Huxley lamented that he and his friends were 'all getting *old*', and noted that Gervas was convalescing from prostate cancer, Harold Nicolson (the politician and husband of Vita Sackville-West) had just had a stroke, and E. M. Forster, whom he was due to meet for drinks, had injured himself after falling off a chair (*SL*, 488).

That autumn in Los Angeles, Huxley learned that the cancer had spread to the glands in his neck and he was forced to cancel a lecture series in October. Despite the inexorable progress of the cancer, Huxley seems to have been in denial about his impending death and never spoke to Laura about it. He had optimistically begun a 'rather long and complicated novel' earlier that year (*LAH*, 947). In a diary entry from 11 November, Isherwood writes:

> Aldous nearly died, a couple of nights ago. Yet he still seems unaware of his condition. He said to Laura that he was worried how he would spend the rest of his life, if he couldn't write: and he implied that he expects to live at least five more years.[40]

Laura confirmed that 'Aldous had not consciously looked at the fact that he might die until the day he died.'[41] For some weeks, Huxley had had difficulty speaking and was subject to racking coughing fits. On 22 November he wrote on a typewriter tablet, 'If I go', and made a stipulation about his life insurance policy. There followed a period of extreme restlessness, with Laura shifting his position in bed to no avail; around 11.30 a.m. he wrote on the tablet: 'Try LSD 100 mmg intramuscular'. Just making the decision, Laura reported, helped to settle him. Back in 1955, when he'd taken mescaline with Laura, he wrote to Osmond: 'Another thing I remember saying and feeling was that I didn't think I should mind dying; for dying must be like this passage from the known (constituted by life-long habits of subject–object existence) to the unknown cosmic fact' (*LAH*, 771). After half an hour, his face began to 'look as it did when he had taken the *moksha*-medicine, when this immense expression of complete bliss and love would come over him'.[42] Laura gave him another 100 mmg of LSD, and spent the next few hours urging him to embrace the light, in the manner of the *Bardo Thödol*, as Huxley had done for Maria. His breathing slowed and he finally died at 5.20 p.m. All those present – Laura, Virginia, Rosalind Rajagopal – agreed 'that this was the most serene, the most beautiful death'.[43]

Epilogue

While Huxley is still best known as the author of *Brave New World*, it is *The Perennial Philosophy*, *The Doors of Perception* and *Island* that have had the most significant impact on the culture in the decades after his death. Huxley's legacy is clearly etched on the counterculture and the Human Potential Movement of the 1960s, the Deep Ecology movement that was established in the 1970s, the New Age movement of the 1980s and 1990s, and the 'spiritual but not religious' demographic that began to emerge in the 1990s and is currently burgeoning in the twenty-first century.

The most immediate beneficiary was the counterculture. Timothy Leary first took psilocybin mushrooms in Mexico in the summer of 1960 and was so galvanized by the experience that he set up the Psilocybin Project at Harvard University, where he was a professor of psychology, to study the effects of the drug. One of his colleagues pressed on him a copy of *The Doors of Perception*, which made a great impression on Leary, who wrote to Huxley to apprise him of the Psilocybin Project. Huxley was lecturing that autumn at MIT and visited Leary in Newton, Massachusetts, where they both took psilocybin.[1] Huxley advised Leary to convince influential psychiatrists, scientists, intellectuals and well-connected businessmen of the benefit of psychedelic drugs, so that they might pave the way for government research grants and the responsible, guided use of psychedelics among the general public. Leary was initially responsive to Huxley's approach but changed his mind after meeting the beat poet Allen Ginsberg, who persuaded him to reject 'Huxley's elitist perspective' in favour of Ginsberg's 'American open-to-the-public approach'.[2] After being fired from Harvard for not teaching his classes, Leary started a psychedelic retreat in Zihuatanejo, Mexico, inspired by Huxley's novel *Island*. In a letter to Osmond, Huxley expressed his dismay with Leary's behaviour: 'why, oh why does he *have* to be such an ass?' (*LAH*, 945). Zihuatanejo was closed by the Mexican authorities in 1963, but this was merely the first of a series of increasingly messianic projects by Leary, and his showboating psychedelic proselytizing helped to create the moral panic that led to LSD being banned in every state by October 1966, fulfilling Huxley's prophecy that widespread use by the general public would lead to prohibition.[3]

One of Huxley's lectures provided the inspiration for the Esalen Institute for alternative spirituality in Big Sur, California. Richard Price, one of the co-founders of Esalen, heard Huxley speak at the University of California, San Francisco Medical Center in 1960. Price told Michael Murphy (the other founder of Esalen) about Huxley's notion of human potentialities and Murphy wrote to Huxley asking if he and Price might visit him when they passed through California in June 1961. Huxley was in London at the time, but suggested that they visit Gerald Heard in Santa Monica, who helped to convince them to go ahead with their plans for Esalen.[4] When the Esalen Institute first opened its doors in September 1962, its catalogue was entitled 'Human Potentialities'. The Human Potential Movement (HPM) came a few years later in 1965 and was the brainchild of Murphy and the writer and educator George Leonard. They hoped that the HPM would combine the political activism of the civil rights movement with an attempt to realize Huxley's human potentialities.[5]

Huxley's emphasis on the need for integration between body and mind in order to facilitate education, not to mention well-being, spiritual fulfilment and so on, was a fundamental tenet of most of the body therapies offered at Esalen, including the

Alexander technique and Rolfing. The transpersonal psychologist Abraham Maslow, who emphasized the psychological nature of religion, was a popular teacher at Esalen and Huxley's human potentialities came to be associated with Maslow's notion of 'self-actualization'. The latter was achieved by creative, gifted individuals who had successfully realized their human potentialities and as a result were prone to 'peak experiences' – transports of happiness, awareness and metaphysical meaning. Maslow was an admirer of Huxley's work, and his mistrust of organized religion and his promotion of a personal spirituality that realized the sacred in one's body and the everyday world were clearly foreshadowed in *Island*.[6]

Huxley also exercised a considerable influence on the New Age movement. He was an early adopter of yoga,[7] meditation and the Alexander technique, all of which would later be identified with the alternative spirituality of the New Age. He practised alternative therapies, such as hypnotism and magnetic passes, as well as acupuncture, the Bates method, dianetics and the E-Therapy pioneered by A. L. Kitselman. Huxley's attempts to reconcile science and spirituality, both in *Island* and throughout his work, would be taken up by later New Age authors, such as Fritjof Capra in *The Tao of Physics* (1975) and Gary Zukav in *The Dancing Wu Li Masters* (1979). Huxley's promotion of the Perennial Philosophy as a highest common factor that united the world religions struck a receptive chord in the New Age, whose proponents rejected institutional religion but adopted certain doctrines, such as karma and reincarnation, from the so-called spiritual supermarket. This eclectic attitude to spirituality is exemplified in *Island*, in which the inhabitants of Pala pick and choose their beliefs and practices from different religious traditions, such as Tantra, Zen and Mahayana Buddhism, rather than subscribing to one. Indeed, they are taught to mistrust dogma and institutional religion, and to form their own subjective experiential spirituality through the sacramental use of *maithuna* and the *moksha*-medicine. New Age culture, despite its subsequent commodification, represented an alternative to mainstream consumer culture. One of the utopian elements of Pala is its isolation from global capitalism: rather than exploiting the island's natural resources, the Palanese live in harmony with nature and take from it only what they need. With the help of the *moksha*-medicine, they are able to apprehend the immanent godhead in the world around them, which inspires a reverent attitude to nature.

This spiritual approach to ecology was something that would be eagerly embraced in the 1970s by the Deep Ecology movement. The latter promoted an ecocentric (as opposed to an anthropocentric) paradigm, in which humans were regarded as but one part of nature and therefore were not accorded an exceptional status. George Sessions and Bill Duvall acknowledged the influence of Huxley on Deep Ecology thinking, and presented *Island* as an exemplary eco-utopia for the movement.[8] For the Palanese, ecology is an integral part of their children's education. The school principal tells Farnaby: 'We shall be permitted to live on this planet only for as long as we treat all nature with compassion and intelligence' (*i*, 212). While the Deep Ecology movement continues to this day, it has been largely eclipsed in the contemporary consciousness by more radical environmental groups, such as Extinction Rebellion (XR). Despite the secular nature of their demands, XR recognize the intersectional possibilities of spirituality and environmental activism. For instance, in the XR Easter protests that took place in London in April 2019, there were a number of 'inter-faith' talks and a vigil that 'combined prayers and songs from Pagan, Christian, Jewish, Muslim and indigenous spiritual traditions'.[9] In the current Anthropocene epoch of climate change and mass extinction, Huxley's work remains highly relevant.

Huxley played a vital role in creating the spiritual but not religious culture that flourishes today. Originally, the adjective 'spiritual' was used as an antonym to the secular, but from the

1970s onwards it came to be used in opposition to institutional religion and culminated in the new category of spiritual but not religious.[10] The widespread disenchantment with organized religion can be seen from a recent Pew survey in which 27 per cent of Americans identified themselves as spiritual but not religious.[11] Various reasons have been posited for this trend. Organized religion can often seem out of kilter with contemporary political concerns, such as equality, the environment, female clergy, abortion and LGBTQ+ issues. In *Island*, the Palanese formulate their own beliefs through the use of the *moksha*-medicine rather than passively accepting outdated theology and ethics.

Finally, Huxley's legacy is clearly legible in psychedelic research, which has started again after a twenty-year moratorium. Huxley's mystical interpretation of the mescaline experience evidently influenced Osmond, for three years after meeting Huxley in 1953, Osmond had coined the word 'psychedelic' (meaning mind-manifesting), in order to connote the spiritual dimensions of mescaline, LSD and psilocybin. In an article the following year, Osmond argued that the term 'psychotomimetic' (psychosis-mimicking) should be abandoned since it overlooked the 'social, philosophical, and religious implications' of these drugs.[12] Inspired by Huxley, Osmond and his colleague Abram Hoffer pioneered 'psychedelic therapy', which involved a single large dose of LSD and a guided trip that made use of a conducive setting, such as music and paintings by Van Gogh, and which achieved good results with alcoholics.[13] Following the United States Federal Controlled Substances Act of 1970, which banned all psychedelic substances and declared them to be 'without medical utility', scientific research in this area ground to a halt.[14] But in the 1990s, with the rise of neuroscience and George Bush's support for the new 'decade of the brain', legal research became possible and a new generation of researchers continued to explore the spiritual dimensions of psychedelic drugs begun by Huxley and Osmond.[15] To cite but one high-profile study at Johns Hopkins Medical School, 67 per cent of the volunteers who took psilocybin in a conducive setting reported mystical-type experiences, with 33 per cent judging the 'psilocybin experience as being the single most spiritually significant experience of his or her life'.[16] Perhaps after all, as Huxley predicted in an essay from 1958, legal psychedelic drugs will lead to a religious revival: 'From being an activity concerned mainly with symbols religion will be transformed into an activity concerned mainly with experience and intuition – an everyday mysticism.'[17] In the twenty-first century, the appetite for spiritual experience can be witnessed in the welter of meditation retreats, ayahuasca holidays, the multi-billion dollar 'shroom boom', the popularity of yoga, tai chi and other mind–body practices, the rise of spiritual communities and centres (Esalen, Findhorn, Damanhur, the Garrison Institute), the spiritual but not religious atmosphere of festivals like Burning Man and of the new breed of activist groups, such as XR and Occupy – now more than ever, the work of Aldous Huxley leads the way.

References

Introduction: Island Universes

1 Gerald Heard, 'The Poignant Prophet', *Kenyon Review*, XXVII/1 (1965),
  p. 63.
2 Christopher Isherwood, *The Sixties: Diaries*, vol. II: *1960–1969*, ed.
  Katherine Bucknell (London, 2010), p. 186.
3 Aldous Huxley, *Texts and Pretexts: An Anthology with Commentaries*
  [1932] (London, 1949), p. 35.
4 See Neil deGrasse Tyson, *Death by Black Hole and Other Cosmic
  Quandaries* (New York, 2007), pp. 44–5.
5 Aldous Huxley, 'Culture and the Individual', in *LSD: The Consciousness-
  expanding Drug*, ed. David Solomon (New York, 1964), p. 46.
6 Laura Huxley, *This Timeless Moment: A Personal View of Aldous Huxley*
  (New York, 1968), p. 144.

1 *Bildung* and *Roman*, 1894–1921

1 See Julian Huxley, *Memories* (Harmondsworth, 1972), p. 64.
2 From the John Chandos interview with Aldous Huxley recorded on
  7 and 11 July 1961, in the Huxley archive of the Harry Ransom Center,
  The University of Texas at Austin.
3 Quoted in Sybille Bedford, *Aldous Huxley: A Biography* (London, 1993), p. 36.
4 Aldous Huxley, *The Art of Seeing* [1942] (London, 1949), p. vi.
5 Quoted in Uwe Rasch, 'Satire in the Making: Aldous Huxley's 1912
  Sketchbook', *Aldous Huxley Annual*, XV (2015), p. 89.
6 In the 1920s Naomi would establish herself as a novelist under her
  married name, Mitchison.

7 See David Bradshaw, '"A Blind Stay-at-home Mole": Huxley at Oxford, 1913–1916', *Aldous Huxley Annual*, XII–XIII (2012–13), p. 196.

8 Quoted in David King Dunaway, *Aldous Huxley Recollected: An Oral History* (New York, 1995), p. 10.

9 See Julian Huxley, *Memories*, p. 97.

10 Bedford, *Aldous Huxley*, p. 40.

11 See David King Dunaway, *Huxley in Hollywood* (New York, 1989); ebook (n.p., 2017), pp. 26–7.

12 See Julian Huxley, *Memories*, pp. 69, 92.

13 See Ronald W. Clark, *The Huxleys* (New York, 1968), p. 168.

14 See W. T. Stace, *Mysticism and Philosophy* (London, 1961), pp. 131–2.

15 See Chad Walsh, 'Pilgrimage to the Perennial Philosophy: The Case of Aldous Huxley', *Journal of Bible and Religion*, XVI/1 (1948), p. 7.

16 Not to be confused with the painter Balthus, the pseudonym of Balthazar Klossowski, who would become notorious for his upskirt portraits of pubescent girls.

17 Quoted in Bradshaw, 'Huxley at Oxford', p. 217.

18 See Miranda Seymour, *Ottoline Morrell: Life on a Grand Scale* (Sevenoaks, 1992), p. 299. Seymour maintains that Maria took sleeping pills while Bedford (p. 80) writes that she swallowed chloride.

19 Ibid., p. 280.

20 Ottoline Morrell, *Ottoline at Garsington: Memoirs of Lady Ottoline Morrell, 1915–1918*, ed. Robert Gathorne-Hardy (London, 1974), p. 203.

21 See Nicholas Murray, *Aldous Huxley: An English Intellectual* (London, 2002), p. 78, and Seymour, *Ottoline Morrell*, p. 374.

22 See Bedford, *Aldous Huxley*, p. 81.

23 See Murray, *Aldous Huxley*, p. 78.

24 Seymour writes that Philip 'claimed that Maria had done her best to seduce him in the autumn' (p. 381), but Philip was a notorious womanizer and it's much more likely that Maria rebuffed his advances.

25 Quoted in Murray, *Aldous Huxley*, p. 72.

26 Quoted ibid., pp. 87–8 (her italics).

27 Quoted ibid., p. 89.

28 Aldous Huxley, *Jonah: Christmas, 1917* (Oxford, 1917), p. 10.

29 John Sutherland, *Mrs Humphry Ward: Eminent Victorian, Pre-eminent Edwardian* (Oxford, 1990), pp. 201, 350.

30 For more on pacifism in Huxley's early work, see Jake Poller, '"These

Maximal Horrors of War": Aldous Huxley, Garsington and the Great War', *Aldous Huxley Annual*, VI (2006), pp. 63–76.

31 See Bedford, *Aldous Huxley*, p. 95.

32 Quoted in Donald Watt, ed., *Aldous Huxley: The Critical Heritage* (London, 1997), p. 42.

33 See Jerome Meckier, 'Aldous Huxley's Modern Myth: "Leda" and the Poetry of Ideas', *ELH*, LVIII/2 (1991), pp. 441–2.

34 Quoted in Julian Huxley, ed., *Aldous Huxley: 1894–1963; A Memorial Volume* (London, 1966), p. 30.

35 Quoted in Watt, *Critical Heritage*, p. 73.

36 For more on *Crome Yellow*, see Jake Poller, 'Crome Yellow', *The Literary Encyclopedia*, 14 August 2009, www.litencyc.com.

37 Morrell, *Ottoline at Garsington*, pp. 215–16.

38 Bedford, *Aldous Huxley*, p. 123.

39 Aldous Huxley, 'Marginalia', *Athenaeum*, 27 August 1920, p. 274.

2 Dangerous Liaisons, 1921–8

1 Anne Chisholm, *Nancy Cunard* (London, 1979), p. 75.

2 Hermione Lee, quoted in David Bradshaw, 'Those Extraordinary Parakeets: Clive Bell and Mary Hutchinson, Part Two', *Charleston Magazine*, XVII (Spring–Summer 1998), p. 7.

3 Quoted in Nicholas Murray, *Aldous Huxley: An English Intellectual* (London, 2002), p. 143.

4 For more on *Antic Hay*, see Jake Poller, 'Aldous Huxley's *Antic Hay*: London in the Aftermath of World War I', *Literary London Journal*, LVIII/2 (2010).

5 Quoted in Donald Watt, ed., *Aldous Huxley: The Critical Heritage* (London, 1997), p. 82.

6 Aldous Huxley, 'Uncle Spencer', in *Little Mexican: Six Stories* (London, 1948), p. 78.

7 A. S. Eddington, *The Nature of the Physical World* (Cambridge, 1929), pp. 277–8.

8 Ibid., p. 259.

9 Ibid., p. 276.

10 Ibid., p. 338.

11 Quoted in Nancy D. Hargrove, 'The Remarkable Relationship of T. S. Eliot and Mary Hutchinson', *Yeats Eliot Review*, xxviii/3–4 (2011), p. 7.

12 Quoted in Margaret C. Ratliff, 'The Correspondence of Mary Hutchinson: A New Look at Bloomsbury, Eliot and Huxley', PhD thesis, The University of Texas at Austin, 1991, p. 210.

13 Aldous Huxley, 'Fashions in Love', in *CE*, vol. ii, p. 346.

14 See David Bradshaw's introduction to *Brave New World* (London, 2004), pp. vii–viii.

15 Quoted in Murray, *Aldous Huxley*, p. 208.

16 See Michael Squires, introduction to *Lady Chatterley's Lover*, ed. Michael Squires (Cambridge, 2002), p. xxiv.

17 See Julian Huxley, *Memories*, p. 153.

18 See Watt, *Critical Heritage*, p. 13.

19 See also Jake Poller, *Aldous Huxley and Alternative Spirituality* (Boston, MA, and Leiden, 2019), pp. 48, 52, 230.

3 Intimations of Technocracy, 1928–33

1 Virginia Woolf, 'Modern Fiction', in *The Essays of Virginia Woolf*, ed. Andrew McNeille, vol. iv (London, 1984), p. 160.

2 See *LAH*, p. 330.

3 Aldous Huxley, 'What, Exactly, Is Modern?', in *CE*, vol. i, pp. 172–3.

4 Aldous Huxley, 'Pascal', in *CE*, vol. ii, pp. 391, 392.

5 D. H. Lawrence, *Apocalypse and the Writings on Revelation*, ed. Mara Kalnins (Cambridge, 1980), p. 149. For more on Huxley's relationship with Lawrence, see Jake Poller, 'The Philosophy of Life-worship: D. H. Lawrence and Aldous Huxley', *D. H. Lawrence Review*, xxxiv–xxxv (2010), pp. 75–91.

6 Aldous Huxley, 'Squeak and Gibber', in *CE*, vol. iii, pp. 145–6.

7 See Harry Price, *Fifty Years of Psychical Research* (London, 1939), p. 107.

8 Aldous Huxley, *The World of Light*, in *Verses and a Comedy: Early Poems, Leda, The Cicadas, The World of Light* (London, 1946), p. 225.

9 For more on Huxley and psychical research, see Jake Poller, 'Beyond the Subliminal Mind: Psychical Research in the Work of Aldous Huxley', *Aries: Journal for the Study of Western Esotericism*, xv (2015), pp. 247–66.

10 Aldous Huxley, 'The Outlook for American Culture: Some Reflections in a Machine Age', in *CE*, vol. III, pp. 188–9.

11 Aldous Huxley, 'Silence Is Golden', in *CE*, vol. II, pp. 20–21.

12 Ibid., p. 23.

13 See Aldous Huxley, 'What Is Happening to Our Population?', in *CE*, vol. III, pp. 402–3.

14 See Aldous Huxley, 'A Note on Eugenics', in *CE*, vol. II, pp. 283–4.

15 See Peter Edgerly Firchow, *The End of Utopia: A Study of Aldous Huxley's 'Brave New World'* (Toronto, 1984), p. 83.

16 This is the phrase Huxley uses in the essay 'What Is Happening to Our Population?', in *CE*, vol. III, p. 400.

17 See Aldous Huxley, 'Pleasures', in *CE*, vol. I, p. 356; 'One and Many', in *CE*, vol. II, p. 318; 'The Outlook for American Culture', in *CE*, vol. III, p. 189; 'The Victory of Art over Humanity', ibid., p. 283.

18 See Jerome Meckier, 'On D. H. Lawrence and Death, Especially Matricide: *Sons and Lovers, Brave New World*, and Aldous Huxley's Later Novels', *Aldous Huxley Annual*, VII (2007), pp. 191–6, and William York Tindall, *Forces in Modern British Literature, 1885–1946* (New York, 1949). For a detailed rebuttal of this position, see Poller, 'The Philosophy of Life-worship', pp. 84–5.

19 This idea can be found in several books by Wells, such as the world states envisaged in *Anticipations* (1902), *A Modern Utopia* (1905) and the Open Conspiracy in *The World of William Clissold* (1926).

20 Aldous Huxley, 'The New Salvation', in *CE*, vol. III, p. 212.

21 Ibid.

22 Following the Wall Street Crash in 1929, unemployment was rising and there was a run on the pound in August that resulted in the collapse of the Labour Party and the formation of an emergency National Government.

23 David Bradshaw, 'Open Conspirators: Huxley and H. G. Wells, 1927–35', in *The Hidden Huxley: Contempt and Compassion for the Masses, 1920–36* (London, 1994), p. 37. For a much more nuanced analysis of Bradshaw's thesis, see Jake Poller, *Aldous Huxley and Alternative Spirituality* (Boston, MA, and Leiden, 2019), pp. 65–70.

24 David Bradshaw, 'Huxley's Slump: Planning, Eugenics, and the "Ultimate Need" of Stability', in *The Art of Literary Biography*, ed. John Batchelor (Oxford, 1995), p. 161.

25 See Aldous Huxley, 1946 foreword to *Brave New World* (London, 2004), p. xxx.

26 See Aldous Huxley, 'On the Charms of History and the Future of the Past', in *CE*, vol. III, pp. 132–5.

27 See Robert S. Baker, *Brave New World: History, Science, and Dystopia* (Boston, MA, 1990), p. 112.

28 Gerald Heard, 'The Poignant Prophet', *Kenyon Review*, XXVII/1 (1965), p. 57.

29 See R. S. Deese, *We Are Amphibians: Julian and Aldous Huxley on the Future of Our Species* (Oakland, CA, 2015), p. 167.

30 H. G. Wells, *The Shape of Things to Come: The Ultimate Revolution* (London, 1935), p. 279.

31 Bradshaw, 'Open Conspirators', p. 37.

32 Quoted in Nicholas Murray, *Aldous Huxley: An English Intellectual* (London, 2002), p. 257.

33 See Roger Luckhurst, *Zombies: A Cultural History* (London, 2015), pp. 22, 25.

34 See Selena Hastings, *Sybille Bedford: An Appetite for Life*, ebook (n.p., 2020), pp. 74–7, 97. See also David King Dunaway, *Huxley in Hollywood* (New York, 1989); ebook (n.p., 2017), pp. 91–2.

35 See Sybille Bedford, *Aldous Huxley: A Biography* (London, 1993), pp. 236–8.

36 Sybille Bedford, *Quicksands: A Memoir* (London, 2005), p. 301.

37 See Donald Watt, ed., *Aldous Huxley: The Critical Heritage* (London, 1997), p. 17.

38 See Bedford, *Aldous Huxley*, p. 252.

39 These sums were calculated with the Bank of England Inflation Calculator and the US Inflation Calculator, using the exchange rate of $1.33 to the pound in December 2018.

40 Aldous Huxley, 'Abroad in England', in *CE*, vol. III, pp. 270–71.

41 Huxley, quoted in J.W.N. Sullivan, *Contemporary Mind: Some Modern Answers* (London, 1934), p. 146.

42 See Bedford, *Aldous Huxley*, p. 278.

43 Quoted in David Bradshaw, 'Huxley and Progressive Education: Daltonism and the Dartington Hall Debacle', *Aldous Huxley Annual*, XV (2015), p. 8.

44 See ibid., pp. 8–14.

45 See Bedford, *Aldous Huxley*, p. 248, where she diplomatically writes that Maria's 'delicate constitution' was 'not helped by not infrequent pregnancies – always interrupted'. See also Stan Lauryssens, *My Brave New World: The Life and Loves of Maria and Aldous Huxley*, ebook (n.p., 2017), a non-fiction novel that he based on the 2,000 letters Maria wrote to her sisters archived in the Albertina Royal Library in Brussels, and in which he reports that Maria had several abortions that resulted in chronic anaemia, and portrays Huxley as indifferent to Maria's protestations of love.

46 Aldous Huxley, *Beyond the Mexique Bay: A Traveller's Journal*, in *CE*, vol. III, p. 569.

47 Bedford, *Aldous Huxley*, p. 273.

48 Lawrence, quoted in Huxley, *Beyond the Mexique Bay*, p. 605.

49 Quoted in David Bradshaw, '"A Blind Stay-at-home Mole": Huxley at Oxford, 1913–1916', *Aldous Huxley Annual*, XII/XIII (2012–13), p. 217.

50 Huxley, *Beyond the Mexique Bay*, pp. 538, 540.

51 Hastings, *Sybille Bedford*, p. 103.

52 See ibid., pp. 103–4.

4 The Oceanic Feeling, 1933–9

1 See Julian Huxley, *Memories* (Harmondsworth, 1972), pp. 96–7.

2 See *LAH*, p. 382.

3 Bedford claims it was either Heard or George Bernard Shaw who made the introduction, while Seymour asserts that it was Morrell. See Sybille Bedford, *Aldous Huxley: A Biography* (London, 1993), p. 312 and Miranda Seymour, *Ottoline Morrell: Life on a Grand Scale* (Sevenoaks, 1992), p. 300, respectively.

4 See F. Matthias Alexander, *The Use of the Self: Its Conscious Direction in Relating to Diagnosis, Functioning and the Control of Reaction* (London, 1932).

5 See *LAH*, p. 400, in which Maria Huxley reports that Huxley began seeing Alexander in the autumn of 1935 and that his technique has had a transformative effect on her husband, curing his insomnia. See also Huxley's letter from March 1936 (*LAH*, p. 402), in which he says that colonic irrigation has cured his insomnia.

6 Letters to H.R.L. Sheppard, 1908–37, Lambeth Palace Library, MS 3745, fol. 122.

7 Huxley claimed that this doctrine of states derived from Blake, and in *Texts and Pretexts* (p. 43), he quoted the following lines from *Jerusalem*:

Descend, O Lamb of God, & take away the imputation of Sin
By the Creation of States & the deliverance of individuals evermore. Amen.
  Thus wept they in Beulah over the Four Regions of Albion:
  But many doubted & despaired & imputed Sin & Righteousness,
To Individuals & not to States, and these Slept in Ulro.

8 See Jerry Wasserman, 'Huxley's Either/Or: The Case for *Eyeless in Gaza*', *NOVEL: A Forum on Fiction*, XIII/2 (1980), p. 191.

9 Ronald W. Clark, *The Huxleys* (New York, 1968), p. 151.

10 Quoted ibid., p. 138.

11 See Bedford, *Aldous Huxley*, p. 296.

12 See Selena Hastings, *Sybille Bedford: An Appetite for Life*, ebook (n.p., 2020), pp. 27, 38.

13 See ibid., p. 74.

14 See ibid., p. 86. For more on *Eyeless in Gaza*, see Jake Poller, 'Eyeless in Gaza', *The Literary Encyclopedia*, 14 October 2009, www.litencyc.com.

15 Laura Huxley, *This Timeless Moment: A Personal View of Aldous Huxley* (New York, 1968), p. 18.

16 Aldous Huxley, 'Pacifism and Philosophy', in *Pacifism and Philosophy: An Aldous Huxley Reader*, ed. William Hetherington (London, 1994), p. 17.

17 Sigmund Freud, *Civilization and Its Discontents*, in *The Freud Reader*, ed. Peter Gay (London, 1995), p. 723.

18 Aldous Huxley, *What Are You Going to Do About It? The Case for Constructive Peace* (London, 1936), p. 32.

19 The archives of the PPU contain records of the Sponsors' Meetings, in which Huxley proved himself an energetic participant. For Huxley's anonymous pacifist pamphlets, see Hetherington, *Pacifism and Philosophy*.

20 Martin Ceadel, *Pacifism in Britain, 1914–1945: The Defining of a Faith* (Oxford, 1980), p. 252.

21 Huxley, *What Are You Going to Do About It?*, p. 31.

22 See Ceadel, *Pacifism in Britain*, p. 262.

23 Cecil Day-Lewis in Watt, *The Critical Heritage*, pp. 274–5.

24 See ibid., pp. 245–71. For more on Huxley, Heard and the PPU, see Jake Poller, *Aldous Huxley and Alternative Spirituality* (Boston, MA, and Leiden, 2019), pp. 150–58.

25 Bedford, *Aldous Huxley*, p. 339.

26 Letters to H.R.L. Sheppard, 1908–37, Lambeth Palace Library, fol. 161.

27 See J. B. Rhine, *Extra-sensory Perception* (Boston, MA, 1997).

28 Aldous Huxley, 'Science Turns to the Supernatural', in *CE*, vol. III, p. 169. See also Huxley's essay 'Mind Reading' in the same volume.

29 See David Ellis, *D. H. Lawrence: Dying Game, 1922–1930* (Cambridge, 1998), pp. 182–3. Lawrence hated the idea of being indebted and in return gave Luhan the manuscript of *Sons and Lovers* (which was worth considerably more than the ranch).

30 See Huxley, 'Goals, Roads, and Contemporary Starting-point', in *CE*, vol. IV, p. 329.

31 See Aldous Huxley, 'Beliefs', ibid., pp. 375, 380.

32 See Aldous Huxley, 'Religious Practices', ibid., pp. 344–50.

33 See Huxley, 'Religious Practices' and 'Beliefs', ibid., pp. 350–51, 375–6.

34 Aldous Huxley, *The Art of Seeing* [1942] (London, 1949), p. 6.

35 See ibid., p. 27.

36 See ibid., pp. 39–40.

37 Ibid., p. vii.

38 Mary Baker Eddy, *Science and Health with Key to Scriptures* [1875] (Boston, 2006), p. 289.

39 J.B.S. Haldane, *The Causes of Evolution* [1932] (New Jersey, 1990), p. 15.

40 See also Daniel Aureliano Newman, '"Education of an Amphibian": Anachrony, Neoteny, and *Bildung* in Huxley's *Eyeless in Gaza*', *Twentieth Century Literature*, LXII/4 (2016), p. 415.

41 Quoted in David King Dunaway, *Huxley in Hollywood* (New York, 1989); ebook (n.p., 2017), p. 161.

42 Ibid., p. 334.

43 Aldous Huxley, 'Personality and the Discontinuity of the Mind', in *CE*, vol. II, p. 265.

5 The Perennial Philosophy, 1939–45

1 Radha Rajagopal Sloss, *Lives in the Shadow with J. Krishnamurti* (London, 1991), p. 183.

2 See H. P. Blavatsky, *The Key to Theosophy* (London, 1889), p. 8.

3 See Mark 4:11, quoted ibid., p. 9.

4 See for instance their co-authored books *Occult Chemistry* (1908), *Man: Whence, How and Whither* (1913) and *The Lives of Alcyone* (1924). For a more detailed account of their work, see Jake Poller, '"Under a glamour": Charles Leadbeater, Annie Besant and Neo-Theosophy', in *The Occult Imagination in Britain, 1875–1947*, ed. Christine Ferguson and Andrew Radford (Abingdon, 2018), pp. 77–93.

5 See Mary Lutyens, *The Life and Death of Krishnamurti* (Brockwood Park, Hampshire, 2003), pp. 7–8.

6 See ibid., p. 11.

7 See ibid., p. 9. Krishnamurti allegedly transcribed these teachings from Koot Hoomi on the astral plane and they were published in the book *At the Feet of the Master* (Adyar, 1910).

8 See ibid., p. 31.

9 Quoted in Pupul Jayakar, *Krishnamurti: A Biography* (San Francisco, CA, 1986), p. 47.

10 See Gregory Tillett, *Elder Brother: A Biography of Charles Webster Leadbeater* (London, 1982), pp. 77–8, 188, 196, 198–9, 200–201, 208.

11 See Lutyens, *Life and Death of Krishnamurti*, pp. 69–70.

12 See ibid., p. 78.

13 For a more granular analysis of Huxley's relationship with Krishnamurti, see Jake Poller, *Aldous Huxley and Alternative Spirituality* (Boston, MA, and Leiden, 2019), pp. 179–203.

14 See Swami Vivekananda, 'Paper on Hinduism', www.advaitaashrama. org, accessed 1 February 2018.

15 Christopher Isherwood, in *Vedanta for the Western World* (London, 1949), p. 1.

16 *The Upanishads*, trans. Juan Mascaró (London, 1965), p. 118 (6:14).

17 Ibid., p. 59 (2:20).

18 Ibid., p. 64 (5:10).

19 Ibid., p. 66 (6:14–15).

20 See Christopher Isherwood, *My Guru and His Disciple* (London, 1981), pp. 4–6.

21 Ibid., p. 50.

22 See Alison Falby, *Between the Pigeonholes: Gerald Heard, 1889–1971* (Newcastle, 2008), pp. 12, 14.

23 See ibid., pp. 12–13, 84.

24 Isherwood, *My Guru*, p. 9.

25 See Sybille Bedford, *Aldous Huxley: A Biography* (London, 1993), p. 371.

26 Quoted ibid., p. 391.

27 See the deleted portion of the *Paris Review* interview with George Wickes and Ray Frazer in box 4, 2009 Aldous Huxley Collection in the Charles E. Young Research Library, UCLA.

28 See Isherwood, *My Guru*, p. 75.

29 Ibid., p. 76.

30 Aldous Huxley, *Grey Eminence* [1941] (London, 2005), p. 243.

31 See ibid., pp. 78, 243.

32 Ibid., pp. 85–6.

33 See ibid., p. 249.

34 See ibid., pp. 265, 272.

35 Ibid., pp. 270–71.

36 Ibid., p. 266.

37 Quoted in Watt, *Critical Heritage*, p. 341.

38 Christopher Isherwood, *Diaries*, vol. I: *1939–1960*, ed. Katherine Bucknell (London, 1996), pp. 202–3.

39 See David King Dunaway, *Huxley in Hollywood* (New York, 1989); ebook (n.p., 2017), p. 89.

40 See ibid.

41 Quoted in Lauryssens, *My Brave New World*.

42 Quoted in Bedford, *Aldous Huxley*, p. 420.

43 See ibid., p. 401.

44 See Watt, *Critical Heritage*, pp. 23–4.

45 See Isherwood, *Diaries*, vol. I, pp. 77–8.

46 See Isherwood, *My Guru*, p. 96, and Falby, *Pigeonholes*, p. 106.

47 See Isherwood, *My Guru*, p. 96.

48 'Trabuco Prospectus', in the 2009 Aldous Huxley Collection of the Charles E. Young Research Library, UCLA.

49 See Franklin Zahn, 'Temporary Monk', www.geraldheard.com, accessed 16 April 2018.

50 See Falby, *Pigeonholes*, p. 109.

51 See Bedford, *Aldous Huxley*, p. 414.

52 Letter from Maria Huxley to Grace Hubble (9 January 1944), in the Hubble Collection, HUB674, Huntington Library, San Marino, CA.

53 William Forthman, 'Memories of Gerald Heard', www.geraldheard. com, accessed 17 April 2018.

54 For more on Heard and Trabuco, see Poller, *Aldous Huxley and Alternative Spirituality*, pp. 166–74.

55 Donald S. Lopez, Jr, foreword to *The Tibetan Book of the Dead*, trans. Lāma Kazi Dawa-Samdup (Oxford, 2000).

56 Many Buddhists do not believe in the existence of a self or soul, so in the *Tibetan Book of the Dead* the phrase 'consciousness principle' is used to denote what survives bodily death.

57 See Jake Poller, 'Beyond the Subliminal Mind: Psychical Research in the Work of Aldous Huxley', *Aries: Journal for the Study of Western Esotericism*, xv (2015), pp. 256–7.

58 Aldous Huxley, introduction to *The Song of God: Bhagavad-Gita*, trans. Swami Pravabhananda and Christopher Isherwood (New York, 1958), p. 13. This was written in 1944 and contains the best account of the Perennial Philosophy, whereas in the book of that name, perhaps because Huxley is offering countless examples of the Perennial Philosophy, he does not elucidate it in his own words as clearly as in the extract above.

59 For a more comprehensive analysis of *The Perennial Philosophy*, see Chapter Three of Poller, *Aldous Huxley and Alternative Spirituality*.

60 Quoted in William James, *Varieties of Religious Experience: A Study in Human Nature* [1902] (New York, 1929), p. 400.

61 Quoted ibid., p. 385.

6 Following the Tao, 1945–54

1 See Sybille Bedford, *Aldous Huxley: A Biography* (London, 1993), p. 446.

2 See Radha Rajagopal Sloss, *Lives in the Shadow with J. Krishnamurti* (London, 1991), pp. 193–7. Sloss claims that Krishnamurti and her mother had an affair that lasted for more than 25 years, and that, in order to preserve the secrecy of the affair as well as the sanctity of Krishnamurti's reputation, Rosalind had two abortions.

3 See *LAH*, p. 537.

4 See David King Dunaway, *Huxley in Hollywood* (New York, 1989); ebook (n.p., 2017), pp. 234, 241.

5 *Papio* is the genus of baboons; a catch-fart is a servant or toady; the verb 'impetrate' means to beseech or beg.

6 The phrase 'malicious animal magnetism' derives from the Christian Science of Mary Baker Eddy, and refers to a malevolent form of willpower that at its most virulent could result in 'mental assassination'. Under the dispensation of Belial, there are 'Satanic Science Practitioners' who excel at 'Malicious Animal Magnetism' (p. 69).

7 See James R. Baker, 'Golding and Huxley: The Fables of Demonic Possession', *Twentieth Century Literature*, XLVI/3 (2000), p. 324.

8 See Jeaneane Fowler, *An Introduction to the Philosophy and Religion of Taoism: Pathways to Immortality* (Brighton, 2005), pp. 110–11.

9 Alan Watts, *Tao: The Watercourse Way* (New York, 1975).

10 Ibid.

11 This is an ironic inversion of the words of St Paul: 'not I, but the grace of God which was with me' (1 Cor. 15:10).

12 See also Jake Poller, *Aldous Huxley and Alternative Spirituality* (Boston, MA, and Leiden, 2019), pp. 241–4.

13 This letter is quoted in full in Lauryssens, *My Brave New World*.

14 David Bradshaw, 'The Flight from Gaza: Aldous Huxley's Involvement with the Peace Pledge Union in the Context of His Overall Intellectual Development', in *Now More Than Ever: Proceedings of the Aldous Huxley Centenary Symposium*, ed. Bernfried Nugel (Frankfurt am Main, 1995), pp. 25–6.

15 See Julian Huxley, *Memories II* (Harmondsworth, 1978), pp. 9–12.

16 Ibid., pp. 125, 138.

17 Max Roser, Hannah Ritchie and Esteban Ortiz-Ospina, 'World Population Growth', www. OurWorldInData.org, 5 January 2020.

18 Huxley, 'The Double Crisis', in *CE*, vol. V, pp. 144–5.

19 This scenario was recently found by James Sexton and published in *Aldous Huxley Annual*, XVII–XVIII (2017–18), pp. 12–75.

20 Aldous Huxley and Christopher Isherwood, *Jacob's Hands: A Fable* (New York, 1998), p. 138.

21 See Laura Huxley, 'To Heal or Not to Heal', introduction ibid., p. ix.

22 See Bedford, *Aldous Huxley*, p. 426.

23 In fact, Jeanne had sold their original house in Sanary during the war, but had purchased another one in preparation for their trip in 1948.

24 See Dorthe Refslund Christensen, 'Scientology', in *Dictionary of Gnosis and Western Esotericism*, ed. Wouter J. Hanegraaff et al. (Leiden, 2006), pp. 1047–8.

25 Quoted in Lauryssens, *My Brave New World*.

26 Dunaway, *Huxley in Hollywood*, p. 304.

27 See Allene Symons, *Aldous Huxley's Hands: His Quest for Perception and the Origin and Return of Psychedelic Science* (Amherst, NY, 2015), pp. 37, 126, 143.

28 See ibid., pp. 153, 206.

29 See Osmond's letters to Huxley in *Psychedelic Prophets: The Letters of Aldous Huxley and Humphry Osmond*, ed. Cynthia Carson Bisbee, Paul Bisbee, Erica Dyck et al. (London, 2018), pp. 13, 201.

30 See Symons, *Aldous Huxley's Hands*, p. 167.

31 See *LAH*, p. 647.

32 See Bedford, *Aldous Huxley*, pp. 509–10.

33 Louis Lewin, *Phantastica: Narcotic and Stimulating Drugs, Their Use and Abuse*, trans. P.H.A. Wirth (New York, 1964), p. 102.

34 See Symons, *Aldous Huxley's Hands*, p. 79.

35 Humphry Osmond, 'Mescaline: On Being Mad', in *Psychedelics: The Uses and Implications of Hallucinogenic Drugs*, ed. Bernard Aaronson and Humphry Osmond (Garden City, NY, 1970), p. 26.

36 Paul Marshall, *Mystical Encounters with the Natural World: Experiences and Explanations* (Oxford, 2005), p. 239.

37 See also Jake Poller, 'Beyond the Subliminal Mind: Psychical Research in the Work of Aldous Huxley', *Aries: Journal for the Study of Western Esotericism*, XV (2015), p. 259.

38 Or, to be more accurate, the Advaita Vedanta as propounded by the American Vedanta Society. Swami Vivekananda had also attempted to incorporate the teachings of *patanjali yoga*, which was rigidly dualistic and world-denying, into the Vedanta Society, thereby making it more ascetic. It should be noted, though, that there are many other expressions of Advaita Vedanta in India that have no connection with the Vedanta Society and these are more life- or world-affirming in their orientation.

7 Death and the *Moksha*-medicine, 1954–63

1 See David King Dunaway, *Huxley in Hollywood* (New York, 1989); ebook (n.p., 2017), p. 343.

2 Huxley uses the variant spelling 'mescalin', which was sometimes used in the first half of the twentieth century.

3 Sybille Bedford, *Aldous Huxley: A Biography* (London, 1993), p. 552.

4 This phrase derives from a short story by H. G. Wells that Huxley adopted as a metaphor for taking psychedelic drugs.

5 Christopher Isherwood, *Diaries*, vol. I: *1939–1960*, ed. Katherine Bucknell (London, 1996), p. 481.

6 See Laura Huxley, *This Timeless Moment: A Personal View of Aldous Huxley* (New York, 1968), pp. 3–6.

7 See Nicholas Murray, *Aldous Huxley: An English Intellectual* (London, 2002), p. 406.

8 Laura Huxley, *This Timeless Moment*, p. 18.

9 See Bedford, *Aldous Huxley*, p. 558.

10 Quoted in *Psychedelic Prophets: The Letters of Aldous Huxley and Humphry Osmond*, ed. Cynthia Carson Bisbee, Paul Bisbee, Erica Dyck et al. (London, 2018), p. 143n.

11 Aldous Huxley, 'D. H. Lawrence', in *CE*, vol. IV, p. 88.

12 See also Jake Poller, *Aldous Huxley and Alternative Spirituality* (Boston, MA, and Leiden, 2019), pp. 246–9.

13 See *Proceedings of the Society for Psychical Research*, L (1956), p. 305, and Jake Poller, 'Beyond the Subliminal Mind: Psychical Research in the Work of Aldous Huxley', *Aries: Journal for the Study of Western Esotericism*, XV (2015), p. 250.

14 See Laura Huxley, *This Timeless Moment*, p. 27.

15 See ibid., p. 10.

16 See Dunaway, *Huxley in Hollywood*, p. 367.

17 Laura Huxley, *This Timeless Moment*, p. 40.

18 Ibid.

19 See his interview with David King Dunaway in the Aldous Huxley Oral History Papers, HM 56903, The Huntington Library, San Marino, CA.

20 Isherwood, *Diaries*, vol. I, p. 709.

21 Quoted in Bisbee et al., *Psychedelic Prophets*, p. 303n.

22 See Laura Huxley, *This Timeless Moment*, pp. 87–9.

23 See Bedford, *Aldous Huxley*, pp. 648–9.

24 Laura Huxley, *This Timeless Moment*, p. 70.

25 Ibid., p. 74.

26 Aldous Huxley Oral History Papers, HM 56903.

27 Aldous Huxley, 'Population Explosion', in *The Human Situation*, ed. Piero Ferrucci (London, 1994), p. 52.

28 For a more detailed analysis of the subject, see Poller, *Aldous Huxley and Alternative Spirituality*, pp. 261–73.

29 Isherwood, *My Guru*, p. 219.

30 John Chandos interview with Aldous Huxley recorded on 7 and 11 July 1961, in the Huxley archive of the Harry Ransom Center, The University of Texas at Austin.

31 Huxley wrote about John Humphrey Noyes and the Oneida Community in the essay 'Domesticating Sex' (1956). Noyes founded a utopian commune at Oneida in New York State, where he introduced the practices of 'Male Continence' and 'Complex Marriage'. The former was a prolonged period of sexual intercourse without ejaculation, which served the practical purpose of contraception and facilitated what Noyes termed 'social magnetism' and mystical contemplation; the latter effectively proscribed monogamy.

32 It should be noted that the Tantric (rather than the Palanese) practice of *maithuna* requires much more than mere mindfulness and a 'special technique' to render it sacred. For more details, see Poller, *Aldous Huxley and Alternative Spirituality*, pp. 255–7.

33 See Jeffrey J. Kripal, *Esalen: America and the Religion of No Religion* (Chicago, IL, 2007), p. 89n7, for this point.

34 See for example Philip Thody, *Aldous Huxley: A Biographical Introduction* (London, 1973), p. 126; and David Bradshaw, 'Aldous Huxley (1894–1963)', who regards the novel as 'perhaps Huxley's most pessimistic book' (*I*, p. xiii).

35 See also Jake Poller, 'Fully Human Being: Aldous Huxley's *Island*, Tantra and Human Potential', *International Journal for the Study of New Religions*, X/1 (2019), pp. 25–47.

36 Laura Huxley, *This Timeless Moment*, p. 289.

37 Quoted ibid., p. 89.

38 Quoted ibid., p. 693.

39 See Julian Huxley, *Memories II*, p. 210.

40 Christopher Isherwood, *The Sixties: Diaries*, vol. II: *1960–1969*, ed. Katherine Bucknell (London, 2010), p. 296.

41 Laura Huxley, *This Timeless Moment*, p. 297.

42   Ibid., p. 306.

43   Letter from Laura Huxley, 8 December 1963, in the Huntington Library
     Collections, CI 1001.

Epilogue

1   See Timothy Leary, *Flashbacks: An Autobiography* (London, 1983),
     pp. 41–3.

2   Ibid., p. 50.

3   For more on Huxley and Leary, see Jake Poller, *Aldous Huxley and
     Alternative Spirituality* (Boston, MA, and Leiden, 2019), pp. 289–94,
     302–4.

4   See Jeffrey J. Kripal, *Esalen: America and the Religion of No Religion*
     (Chicago, IL, 2007), pp. 85–6.

5   Murphy and Leonard's concept of latent human potentialities was
     slightly different from Huxley's in that it included paranormal powers,
     such as telepathy, which they believed would arise as a result of
     spiritual evolution. See Poller, *Aldous Huxley and Alternative Spirituality*,
     pp. 261–74.

6   See Kripal, *Esalen*, pp. 135, 148–50.

7   While living in Wrightwood after the Second World War,
     Krishnamurti gave Huxley and Maria lessons in hatha yoga, which
     Krishnamurti had learnt from B.K.S. Iyengar.

8   See George Sessions and Bill Devall, *Deep Ecology: Living as if Nature
     Mattered* (Layton, UT, 1985), pp. 170–71.

9   Stefan Skrimshire, 'Extinction Rebellion and the New Visibility of Religious
     Protest', *openDemocracy*, www.opendemocracy.net, 12 May 2019.

10   See Boaz Huss, 'Spirituality: The Emergence of a New Cultural
     Category and Its Challenge to the Religious and the Secular', *Journal of
     Contemporary Religion*, XXIX/1 (2014), p. 50.

11   See Michael Lipka and Claire Gecewicz, 'More Americans Now
     Say They're Spiritual but Not Religious', www.pewresearch.org,
     6 September 2017.

12   Humphry Osmond, 'A Review of the Clinical Effects of
     Psychotomimetic Agents', in *LSD: The Consciousness-expanding Drug*,
     p. 135.

13 See Abram Hoffer, 'Treatment of Alcoholism with Psychedelic Therapy', in *Psychedelics: The Uses and Implications of Hallucinogenic Drugs,* ed. Bernard Aaronson and Humphry Osmond (Garden City, NY, 1970), pp. 360–61. Hoffer reported that 50 per cent of the alcoholics they treated never drank again.

14 Quoted in Dana Sawyer, '"A Gratuitous Grace": An Up-to-date Assessment of Aldous Huxley's Psychedelic Mysticism', in *Aldous Huxley and Self-realization: His Concept of Human Potentialities, His Techniques for Actualizing Them and His Views of Their Social Consequences*, ed. Dana Sawyer, Julian Piras and Uwe Rasch (Zurich, 2019), p. 224.

15 See ibid., p. 225.

16 R. R. Griffiths, W. A. Richards, U. McCann and R. Jesse, 'Psilocybin Can Occasion Mystical-type Experiences Having Substantial and Sustained Personal Meaning and Spiritual Significance', *Psychopharmacology*, CLXXXVII/3 (2006), pp. 276–7.

17 Aldous Huxley, 'Drugs That Shape Men's Minds', in *CE*, vol. VI, p. 303.

Select Bibliography

Works by Huxley

The Burning Wheel (1916)
Jonah (1917)
The Defeat of Youth (1918)
Leda (1920)
Limbo: Six Stories and a Play (1920)
Crome Yellow (1921)
Mortal Coils (1922)
Antic Hay (1923)
On the Margin (1923)
Little Mexican: Six Stories (1924)
Along the Road (1925)
Those Barren Leaves (1925)
Two or Three Graces (1926)
Jesting Pilate (1926)
Proper Studies (1927)
Point Counter Point (1928)
Do What You Will (1929)
Arabia Infelix (1929)
Brief Candles (1930)
Music at Night (1931)
The World of Light (1931)
The Cicadas (1931)
Brave New World (1932)
Texts and Pretexts (1932)
Beyond the Mexique Bay: A Traveller's Journal (1934)
Eyeless in Gaza (1936)
What Are You Going to Do About It? The Case for Constructive Peace (1936)

The Olive Tree (1936)
Ends and Means (1937)
After Many a Summer (1939)
Grey Eminence (1941)
The Art of Seeing (1942)
Time Must Have a Stop (1944)
The Perennial Philosophy (1945)
Ape and Essence (1948)
Themes and Variations (1950)
The Devils of Loudun (1952)
The Doors of Perception (1954)
The Genius and the Goddess (1955)
Adonis and the Alphabet (1956)
Heaven and Hell (1956)
Brave New World Revisited (1958)
Island (1962)
Literature and Science (1963)

Posthumous Works

Bisbee, Cynthia Carson, Paul Bisbee, Erica Dyck, et al., *Psychedelic Prophets: The Letters of Aldous Huxley and Humphry Osmond* (London, 2018)
Bradshaw, David, ed., *The Hidden Huxley: Contempt and Compassion for the Masses, 1920–36* (London, 1994)
Ferrucci, Piero, ed., *The Human Situation* (London, 1994)
Hetherington, William, ed., *Pacifism and Philosophy: An Aldous Huxley Reader* (London, 1994)
Huxley, Aldous, and Christopher Isherwood, *Jacob's Hands: A Fable* (New York, 1998)
Sexton, James, ed., *Selected Letters of Aldous Huxley* (Chicago, IL, 2007)
—, and Robert S. Baker, *Aldous Huxley: Complete Essays*, 6 vols (Chicago, IL, 2000–2002)
Smith, Grover, ed., *The Letters of Aldous Huxley* (London, 1969)
Watt, Donald, ed., *The Collected Poetry of Aldous Huxley* (London, 1971)

Works on Huxley

Baker, James R., 'Golding and Huxley: The Fables of Demonic Possession',
    Twentieth Century Literature, XLVI/3 (2000), pp. 311–27
Baker, Robert S., *Brave New World: History, Science, and Dystopia* (Boston,
    MA, 1990)
Bedford, Sybille, *Aldous Huxley: A Biography* [1973–4] (London, 1993)
Bradshaw, David, '"A Blind Stay-at-home Mole": Huxley at Oxford,
    1913–1916', *Aldous Huxley Annual*, XII–XIII (2012–13), pp. 195–222
—, 'The Flight from Gaza: Aldous Huxley's Involvement with the
    Peace Pledge Union in the Context of His Overall Intellectual
    Development', in *Now More Than Ever: Proceedings of the Aldous
    Huxley Centenary Symposium*, ed. Bernfried Nugel (Frankfurt am
    Main, 1995), pp. 9–27
—, 'Huxley and Progressive Education: Daltonism and the Dartington Hall
    Debacle', *Aldous Huxley Annual*, XV (2015), pp. 1–20
—, 'Huxley's Slump: Planning, Eugenics, and the "Ultimate Need" of
    Stability', in *The Art of Literary Biography*, ed. John Batchelor (Oxford,
    1995), pp. 151–71
—, Introduction, *Brave New World* (London, 2004), pp. v–xv
Clark, Ronald W., *The Huxleys* (New York, 1968)
Deese, R. S., *We Are Amphibians: Julian and Aldous Huxley on the Future of
    Our Species* (Oakland, CA, 2015)
Dunaway, David King, *Huxley in Hollywood* (New York, 1989)
—, *Aldous Huxley Recollected: An Oral History* (New York, 1995)
Firchow, Peter Edgerly, *The End of Utopia: A Study of Aldous Huxley's 'Brave
    New World'* (Toronto, 1984)
Heard, Gerald, 'The Poignant Prophet', *Kenyon Review*, XXVII/1 (1965),
    pp. 49–70
Huxley, Julian, ed., *Aldous Huxley: 1894–1963; A Memorial Volume* (London,
    1966)
—, *Memories*, 2 vols (Harmondsworth, 1972–8)
Huxley, Laura, *This Timeless Moment: A Personal View of Aldous Huxley*
    (New York, 1968)
Lauryssens, Stan, *Mijn heerlijk nieuwe wereld, leven en liefdes van Maria Nys-
    Huxley* (Antwerp, 2001); Eng. trans. as *My Brave New World: The Life
    and Loves of Maria and Aldous Huxley*, ebook (n.p., 2017)

Meckier, Jerome, 'Aldous Huxley's Modern Myth: "Leda" and the Poetry of Ideas', *ELH*, LVIII/2 (1991), pp. 439–69.

—, 'On D. H. Lawrence and Death, Especially Matricide: *Sons and Lovers, Brave New World*, and Aldous Huxley's Later Novels', *Aldous Huxley Annual*, VII (2007), pp. 185–221

Murray, Nicholas, *Aldous Huxley: An English Intellectual* (London, 2002)

Newman, Daniel Aureliano, '"Education of an Amphibian": Anachrony, Neoteny, and *Bildung* in Huxley's *Eyeless in Gaza*', *Twentieth Century Literature*, LXII/4 (2016), pp. 403–28

Poller, Jake, *Aldous Huxley and Alternative Spirituality* (Boston, MA, and Leiden, 2019)

—, 'Aldous Huxley's *Antic Hay*: London in the Aftermath of World War I', *Literary London Journal*, VIII/2 (2010)

—, 'Beyond the Subliminal Mind: Psychical Research in the Work of Aldous Huxley', *Aries: Journal for the Study of Western Esotericism*, XV (2015), pp. 247–66

—, 'Fully Human Being: Aldous Huxley's *Island*, Tantra and Human Potential', *International Journal for the Study of New Religions*, X/1 (2019), pp. 25–47

—, 'The Philosophy of Life-worship: D. H. Lawrence and Aldous Huxley', *D. H. Lawrence Review*, XXXIV–XXXV (2010), pp. 75–91

—, '"These Maximal Horrors of War": Aldous Huxley, Garsington and the Great War', *Aldous Huxley Annual*, VI (2006), pp. 63–76

Rasch, Uwe, 'Satire in the Making: Aldous Huxley's 1912 Sketchbook', *Aldous Huxley Annual*, XV (2015), pp. 21–120

Sawyer, Dana, *Aldous Huxley: A Biography* (New York, 2002)

—, '"A Gratuitous Grace": An Up-to-date Assessment of Aldous Huxley's Psychedelic Mysticism', in *Aldous Huxley and Self-realization: His Concept of Human Potentialities, His Techniques for Actualizing Them and His Views of Their Social Consequences*, ed. Dana Sawyer, Julian Piras and Uwe Rasch (Zurich, 2019), pp. 217–42

Symons, Allene, *Aldous Huxley's Hands: His Quest for Perception and the Origin and Return of Psychedelic Science* (Amherst, NY, 2015)

Thody, Philip, *Aldous Huxley: A Biographical Introduction* (London, 1973)

Walsh, Chad, 'Pilgrimage to the Perennial Philosophy: The Case of Aldous Huxley', *Journal of Bible and Religion*, xvi/1 (1948), pp. 3–12

Wasserman, Jerry, 'Huxley's Either/Or: The Case for *Eyeless in Gaza*', NOVEL: *A Forum on Fiction*, xiii/2 (1980), pp. 132–48

Watt, Donald, ed., *Aldous Huxley: The Critical Heritage* (London, 1997)

Acknowledgements

First of all, I'd like to thank my colleague kitt price for recommending me to write this book. Many thanks to Vivian Constantinopoulos for her help and advice, especially during the coronavirus lockdown, and to Alex Ciobanu and Amy Salter at Reaktion Books. Dana Sawyer, despite having written an excellent biography of Huxley himself, has been extremely helpful and enthusiastic about my book, and I have benefited tremendously from our ongoing discussions of Huxley and his spiritual interests. Dana put me in touch with Jon Monday and Swami Vedamritananda from the Vedanta Society of Southern California, who graciously provided me with the photos of Huxley and Swami Prabhavananda. James Sexton has also been splendidly generous with his time and expertise, and has shared with me much recherché archival material I wouldn't have been able to access otherwise. I'm grateful to Jeffrey Kripal for inviting me to the 'Religion of No Religion' symposium at the Esalen Institute in December 2019, where I gave a paper that covered many of the issues I write about in the epilogue. Jeff's work on Huxley has been a big inspiration and deserves a much wider readership. Thanks also to Uwe Rasch, who located some great (and more importantly free) photos of Huxley in the Huntington Library collection. I'd like to thank all the archivists, academics and librarians who helped me to obtain permissions for the photos of Huxley and his friends, including Peter Huestis at the National Gallery of Art, Washington; Bethany Hamblen and Seamus Perry at Balliol College; Jessica Tubis at the Beinecke Rare Book and Manuscript Library; and Beth Owens at the Cleveland Museum of Art.

For permission to quote from Huxley's works, I'm grateful to James W. Spisak at the Aldous and Laura Huxley Literary Trust and to Cora Markowitz at Georges Borchardt, Inc., Literary Agency.

Photo Acknowledgements

The author and publishers wish to express their thanks to the below sources of illustrative material and/or permission to reproduce it. Some locations of artworks are also given below, in the interest of brevity:

Alfred Stieglitz Collection, National Gallery of Art, Washington, DC: p. 76; Beinecke Rare Book and Manuscript Library, Yale University, New Haven, CT: pp. 57 (YCAL MSS 424), 144 (YCAL MSS 196); photo Bettmann/ Getty Images: p. 40; The Cleveland Museum of Art, OH: p. 131; © Estate of Vanessa Bell (all rights reserved), DACS 2021/photo © Tate: p. 50; The Huntington Library, San Marino, CA: pp. 115 (HUB 1067), 118 (HUB 1069); from Leonard Huxley, *The Life and Letters of Thomas Henry Huxley*, vol. II (London, 1900): p. 16; Library of Congress, Prints and Photographs Division, Washington, DC: p. 106; courtesy The Masters and Fellows, Balliol College, Oxford (photos F. F. Urquhart): pp. 21, 24; Pictorial Press Ltd/Alamy Stock Photo: p. 97; courtesy photos © Vedanta Society of Southern California, used with permission: pp. 109, 111; Wellcome Collection (CC BY 4.0): p. 19.